PRINCIPLES FOR PERSONAL GROWTH

MAKE MORE PROGRESS AND FEEL GOOD MORE OFTEN

Adam Khan

Published by: YouMe Works
Printed in the United States

Contact the author or publisher
at www.youmeworks.com

This book is a revised version of *Self-Help Stuff That Works.*

Editor and consultant for the book: Klassy Evans

ISBN-13: 978-0962465697
ISBN-10: 0962465690

Table of Contents

THE WORK SECTION

THE PEOPLE SECTION

Acknowledgment

FOR MANY YEARS I sat in the back of the room running the recording machinery while Klassy Evans gave her talks and workshops. I recorded her on countless videotapes and audiotapes, and while I was doing this, I absorbed a lot. Many of her ideas and principles made it into this book, and I owe Klassy a great deal for those, among other things. Klassy has been my editor, my collaborator, and my best friend for 29 years.

I have decided to give a portion of the proceeds of this book to her. In fact, I'm giving *all* the proceeds to her, because I married her and she takes care of the money.

Introduction

IF I WERE SITTING DOWN to read this book for the first time, a question on my mind would be: "What will I gain by reading this book?"

The answer is: You will gain a large number of ideas you can *apply* — practical ideas that will help you make your circumstances better. And you will get those ideas separately: Each chapter is independent from the others and can be read in any order.

This book covers a broad spectrum of feelings and situations, so at any given time and for any given circumstance, you could profitably look in here and find something useful — some principle you could apply that would improve your situation or your attitude toward it.

The main thing you'll get from this book is a collection of methods you can use to direct your actions more effectively. For example, if you need to handle a troublemaker at work and what you're doing isn't working, you'll find out why on page 156. And you'll find out what *does* work. The ideas in this book will help you direct your actions so that the things you *want* to happen will be more *likely* to happen.

Principles For Personal Growth is a major revision of the book, *Self-Help Stuff That Works*. I removed seven chapters and added nineteen new ones, as well as doing some updating and editing.

Most of the chapters in this book are a collection of articles I wrote for my column *Adam Khan on Positive Living* in the newsletter *At Your Best*, published by Rodale Press.

When I decided to compile them into a book, they naturally arranged themselves into three categories: attitude, work, and relationships with people. There were some odd exceptions — a few articles on how to make changes in general — and I added one or two to each section to help you translate the ideas into real improvement in the quality of your life.

Are you ready to begin? Okay, but we have one more thing to cover: How to get the most out of this book — the subject of the next chapter.

All of us are self-made, but only the successful will admit it.

— Earl Nightingale

How to Use This Book

THINK OF THIS BOOK as an all-you-can-eat buffet where you pick and choose what you want for now. You can come back again for more at some other time. It is impossible for you to digest the contents of this book in one reading — there is too much here. Please reread and remember that sentence. It is important.

I've deliberately packed this book with powerful, helpful, practical tools in a highly condensed form. This isn't something to read and be finished with. Think of it more like a reference book or a toolbox — something you keep around to use when you need it.

Since the chapters are in no particular order, you can browse around the book until you find something that sparks your interest and read that, leaving the rest until later.

Even if you read straight through the book, some chapters will strike you as especially relevant — they'll answer a current need or situation in your life. When that happens, copy the principle (stated at the end of each chapter) onto a card and carry the card with you for a few days or weeks or even months, concentrating on putting that principle into practice.

Then come back to the book and find another principle or two to practice for a while. Don't try to practice too many at a time — one or two, maybe three at the most.

Or browse the book before you go to bed each night to find a principle you want to practice the next day. Write the principle on a card, and start practicing it first thing in the morning.

Another good use for the book is to refer to it when you're down. When you feel stressed or frustrated or worried or any negative emotion, leaf through the book looking for a chapter that can help you.

As you read, keep a highlighter handy and mark passages that have special meaning for you.

If you'd like to absorb this material in greater depth, I recommend the ARENA process (see page 331). Jim Wales, a professor at Mesa College in San Diego, has been using this book in his course, *Life Skills and Personal Adjustment.* And Wales created ARENA to improve his students' ability to help this information make a difference in their lives.

READING THIS BOOK once wouldn't come *close* to maximizing its value. If you read this book start to finish this week, a year from now you will have forgotten almost all of it. At that time you may be in serious need of an attitude adjustment, but the principle on page 84 is likely to have been buried in a year's worth of new information and memories, stashed somewhere in the back of your mind, unavailable to you.

The things we learn are not etched in stone. They are stored in a gooey organ. And you use that organ — your brain — every day. New ideas and experiences pass through your brain all the time, so what you know fades and is less available to your working memory — except what you use repeatedly. That's why I recommend referring to this book when you're down. It makes a difference. I do it myself and I wrote the book!

Use a principle enough times, and it will become a permanent part of your character. But in the meantime, refer to the book when you need it. And consult it when you want to help your friends. This book was made to be *used*. So let's get to it.

The spirit of self-help is the root of all genuine growth in the individual; and, exhibited in the lives of many, it constitutes the true source of national vigor and strength. Help from without is often enfeebling in its effect, but help from within invariably invigorates.

— Samuel Smiles (excerpted from his book Self-Help, the first book of its kind, published in 1859)

THE ATTITUDE SECTION

Optimism

IT'S AN AGE-OLD BATTLE. Pessimists think optimists are foolish; optimists think pessimists make themselves unnecessarily miserable. A lot of research has been done on this issue in the last forty years. Have we answered the question yet? Is the glass half-full or half-empty?

Martin Seligman, PhD, and his colleagues at the University of Pennsylvania found that optimistic people are happier than pessimists. When something bad happens, optimists think of it as temporary, limited in its effect, and not entirely their fault. Pessimists do the opposite. They consider the setback to be permanent, far-reaching and all their fault. There are varying degrees of this, of course; it's not black or white. Most people fall somewhere between the two extremes.

The main difference between optimists and pessimists is how they explain setbacks to themselves. Using these definitions, researchers find that optimism contributes to good health and pessimism contributes to illness.

In several large scale, long-term, carefully controlled experiments, Seligman discovered that optimists are more successful than pessimists — optimistic politicians win more elections, optimistic students get better grades, optimistic athletes win more contests, optimistic salespeople make more money.

Why would this be so? Because optimism and pessimism both tend to be self-fulfilling prophecies. If you think a setback is permanent, why would you try to change it? Pessimistic explanations tend to make you feel defeated — making you *less* likely to take constructive action. Optimistic explanations, on the other hand, make you *more* likely to act. If you think what caused the setback could be fixed, you're apt to try to do something about it, and *because* you take action, you *make* it temporary. It becomes a self-fulfilling prophecy.

Seligman and his research team tested the swim team of the University of California at Berkeley to find out who were optimists and who were pessimists. Then they created a setback for the team members: The coach told each swimmer his time after he finished a heat, but the coach didn't give the swimmer an accurate time — he gave a time much slower than the swimmer's real time.

How did the swimmers respond to this setback? Seligman says, "The optimists responded by swimming their next heat faster; the pessimists went slower on their next heat."

Optimists *fight back* when they hit a setback. They are resilient in the face of the rejections and disappointments we all face fairly regularly in life. Optimists pick themselves up quickly and go on. They bounce back.

Pessimists succumb. *They give up.* They get depressed or apathetic. They throw in the towel and let life run them over. And the only thing that separates optimists from pessimists is *the way they think* — called their "explanatory style." When optimists have setbacks:

1. They assume the problem or its consequences won't last very long.

2. They don't indulge in self-blame. Instead they look to see if there's anything they could do to prevent the same thing from happening in the future.

3. They don't jump to the conclusion that this setback will ruin everything. An optimist will try to see how much of their lives the setback *won't* affect.

YOU CAN BECOME more optimistic by practicing these three ways of thinking about setbacks, and every inch you move toward optimism means another inch of resiliency. It means you'll bounce back sooner from the inevitable setbacks of life. It means you'll have greater personal strength and persistence. It means more of your life will go the way you want it to go.

Look at those three optimistic ways of thinking. Find the one you're weakest in and work on it. Practice on the little setbacks you experience — the small disappointments, frustrations, annoyances, interruptions in your everyday experience. Learn to think the optimistic way. Practice until that way of thinking is habitual.

When it seems like life is trying to beat you down, you can fight back with optimistic thoughts.

And if you do, you will not only be happier and more successful, you will also be physically *healthier* (this just keeps getting better, doesn't it?). When Chris Peterson was teaching a class in abnormal psychology at Virginia Tech, he told his students to fill out an Attributional Style Questionnaire — a carefully designed test that determines a person's level of optimism and pessimism. The students also answered questions about their general health, including how often they went to a doctor.

Peterson followed the health of his students the following year and discovered that the pessimists had *twice* as many infectious diseases and made *twice* as many trips to the doctor as the optimists.

Later, Martin Seligman and two of his colleagues, using interviews and blood tests, found that optimists have better immune activity than pessimists. Studies by other researchers show the same thing. Why? Because of a simple fact: "Pessimistic individuals," as Seligman writes, "get depressed more easily and more often."

When a person is depressed, certain brain hormones become depleted, creating a chain of biochemical events that slow down the activity of the immune system. For example, two vital components of your immune system are T cells and NK cells.

> **T cells** recognize invaders (like viruses) and make more copies of themselves to kill off the invaders. Pessimists' T cells don't multiply as quickly as optimists', allowing invaders to get the upper hand.
>
> **NK cells** circulate in the blood and kill whatever they come across that they identify as foreign (like cancer cells). Pessimists' NK cells can identify foreign entities, but they don't destroy them as well as the optimists' NK cells.

OPTIMISTS ALSO LOOK at information in more depth to find out what they can do about the risk factors. In a study by Lisa Aspinwall, PhD, at the University of Maryland, subjects read health-related information on cancer and other topics. She discovered that optimists spent more time than pessimists reading the severe risk material and they remembered more of it.

"These are people," says Aspinwall, "who aren't sitting around wishing things were different. They believe in a better outcome, and that whatever measures they take will help them to heal." In other words, instead of having their heads in the clouds, optimistic people *look*. They do more than look, they *seek*. They aren't afraid to look into the situation *because* they're optimistic. Thus, for yet another reason, optimists are likely to be healthier.

The best news is what research has shown repeatedly: Anyone can become more optimistic with effort. And every effort you make to keep an optimistic attitude will reward you with a stronger immune system. So you will enjoy better health. And it is also true that the better your health, the easier it is to maintain an optimistic outlook.

Pessimistic people have one advantage: In some situations, they see reality more accurately. It's the attitude to adopt if you're thinking of attempting something risky or dangerous. But after a setback has occurred, pessimism will not help you. And one of the biggest counts *against* pessimism is that it causes depression. Or, more accurately, pessimism sets up the condition for depression to occur. One bad setback can knock a pessimist into the pit.

Since depression costs this country more per year than heart disease (the nation's number one killer), pessimism has serious side effects. It's kind of a booby-prize for a pessimist to be able to say, "Yes, but I saw reality more accurately."

The good news is that a pessimist can learn to be an optimist. Pessimists can learn to see the temporary aspects of setbacks. They can be more specific about the effects of it, they can learn not to take all the blame and they can learn to take credit for the good they do. All it takes is practice. Optimism is simply a way of thinking about good and bad; it's a cognitive skill anyone can learn.

So, what about the age-old conflict? Is the glass half-full or half-empty? Our best answer is that the glass is both half-full *and* half-empty, but *you're* much better off if you think of it as half-full.

When you hit a setback in life:
Assume the problem or its consequences won't last long, don't jump to the conclusion that this setback will ruin everything (look to see what *isn't* affected), and don't indulge in self-blame but instead see how you might prevent the same problem in the future.

When something good happens:
Consider the possibility that its effects permanent, see how much of your life is affected, and see how much of it you can honestly take credit for.

Optimism is essential to achievement and it is also the foundation of courage and true progress.

— *Nicholas M. Butler*

What I've really learned over time is that optimism is a very, very important part of leadership.

— *Bob Iger*

Master the Art of Making Meaning

YOUR MIND IS a meaning-making machine. Without even trying, you "know" what things mean, at least most of the time. When someone treats you "rudely," for example, your mind interprets that. It makes some meaning out of it. And it's completely automatic. That is, you don't stop and think about it. You don't *try* to make an interpretation. It happens without any effort on your part.

The meanings you make affect the way you feel and determine how you interact with people and circumstances. The interpretations you make about the events in your life have a significant influence on the amount of stress you experience in your day.

For example, let's say someone cuts you off on the freeway. And let's further postulate, just for fun, that your automatic interpretation is: "What a jerk." The interpretation would probably make you upset, at least a little bit. But realize that it doesn't feel like you're making the *interpretation* "What a jerk." The way it feels to you is that your assessment of the person is obvious, and anyone in their right mind would make the same assessment in the same circumstances. But believe it or not, your interpretation was your own doing, and it wasn't the only possible interpretation you could have made.

The important thing about this is that your interpretations change the way you feel, and those feelings change the way you interact with the world.

The good news is: You're not stuck with the interpretations your mind makes automatically. You can come up with new ones. You wouldn't marry the first person you met after puberty, would you? You wouldn't take a job at the first place you saw a "Help Wanted" sign, would you? Well, you don't have to use the first interpretation that pops into your head, either.

In the example above, the possible ways to interpret someone cutting you off are virtually unlimited. How about this one: The person had unexpected car trouble and now is running terribly late to an important appointment. If the driver is a woman, maybe she's in labor and needs to get to a hospital *now.* If it's a man, maybe he was called at work and told his wife is in labor. Maybe his brakes went out. Maybe he's having heart trouble.

I know we are just making things up, but "He's a thoughtless, inconsiderate bastard" is made up too. None of those interpretations are better than any others in an absolute way because we don't know what the truth is. But which one leaves you able to go on about your day feeling fine? Or, if it's a situation that keeps repeating itself and requires action, which interpretation would most likely help you successfully deal with the situation?

Challenge yourself. Don't settle for the first interpretation that comes to mind. Say to yourself, "Okay, it *might* mean that...what *else* could it mean? What's *another* way to interpret this?" You will feel better, treat people better, and handle situations better. Do you know what this could mean to you? You tell me.

Come up with alternative ways of interpreting an event.

Brighter Future? Sounds Good!

A BRANCH OF PSYCHOLOGY called neurolinguistic programming has made an interesting and useful discovery: You can change *the way* you remember things without changing *what* you remember, and it will change your feelings. For example, if a visual memory makes you sad whenever you think about it, you can make your mental picture of it smaller and dimmer, and when you do, the memory won't make you as sad. Since you haven't changed the *content* of the memory, you haven't lost any information. You've simply made it less painful.

When you visually remember a pleasant memory, you can make the picture more colorful and the memory will give you even more intense good feelings. You can also make your pictures of the future brighter, wider, deeper, or you can bring the images closer. Changes like these can make you feel different — even when the *content* of the picture remains the same.

These are general guidelines. Experiment to find out what will work for a particular image. For a few people, making an exciting picture brighter makes the feelings *less* intense. And for some kinds of pictures, increasing the brightness would cause the feelings to become less intense — for example, a romantic memory.

What is true for visual images also applies to the way you talk to yourself. For example, if you have trouble motivating yourself, try changing the tone of voice you use when you speak to yourself. Some people order themselves around. The voice they use to talk to themselves is harsh and commanding. You may be saying perfectly sensible things to yourself, but listening to yourself being bossy can have the same effect as listening to someone *else* being bossy: It can make you want to rebel. Change your tone to friendly or seductive, and you might feel more motivated.

When you tell yourself, "I can do it," fill your internal voice with enthusiasm and back it up with inspiring music. The possibilities are virtually endless.

The important thing to understand is that the *way* you represent your internal sounds and images has an impact, and you have quite a bit of control over the way you represent them. You can change the way you do it deliberately, and when you do, it will change your feelings, which will change your actions, which will change the world around you.

Change the details of your thoughts.

When you want new results, it requires new thinking.

— Richard Bandler

Brains aren't designed to get results; they go in directions. If you know how the brain works you can set your own directions. If you don't, then someone else will.

— Richard Bandler

Adrift

IN 1982 STEVEN CALLAHAN was crossing the Atlantic alone in his sailboat when it struck something and sank. He was out of the shipping lanes and floating in a life raft, alone. His supplies were few. His chances were slim. Yet when three fishermen found him *seventy-six days later* (the longest anyone has ever survived in an inflatable life raft alone), he was alive — much skinnier than he was when he started, but alive.

His account of how he survived is fascinating. His ingenuity — how he managed to catch fish, how he fixed his solar still (evaporates sea water to make fresh) — is very interesting.

But the thing that caught my eye was how he managed to keep himself going when all hope seemed lost, when there seemed no point in continuing the struggle, when he was suffering greatly, when his life raft was punctured and after more than a week struggling with his weak body to fix it, it was still leaking air and wearing him out to keep pumping it up. He was starved. He was desperately dehydrated. He was thoroughly exhausted. Giving up would have seemed the only sane option.

When people survive these kinds of circumstances, they do something with their minds that gives them the courage to keep going. Many people in similarly desperate circumstances give in or go mad. Something the survivors do with their thoughts helps them find the guts to carry on in spite of overwhelming odds.

"I tell myself I can handle it," wrote Callahan in his narrative. "Compared to what others have been through,

I'm fortunate. I tell myself these things over and over, building up fortitude..."

I wrote that down after I read it. It struck me as something important. And I've told myself the same thing when my own goals seemed far off or when my problems seemed too overwhelming. And every time I've said it, I have always come back to my senses.

The truth is, our circumstances are only bad *compared* to something better. But others *have* been through much worse. I've read enough history to know you and I are lucky to be where we are and *when* we are, no matter how bad it seems to us compared to our fantasies. It's a sane thought and worth thinking.

So here, coming to us from the extreme edge of survival, are words that can give us strength. Whatever you're going through, tell yourself you can handle it. Compared to what others have been through, you're fortunate. Tell this to yourself over and over, and it will help you get through the rough spots with a little more fortitude.

Tell yourself you can handle it.

...everything can be taken from a man but one thing: the last of the human freedoms — to choose one's attitude in any given set of circumstances...

— *Viktor Frankl*

Maybe It's Good

I HAD DONE A LOT OF WALKING in the previous two days and my feet hurt. Of course, I didn't like it. Anybody would agree that having sore feet is a *bad* thing. It could be a sign I'm getting old.

"But maybe it's good," I said to myself, "In fact, maybe it's *perfect.* The pain might be the sensation of strengthening the bones in my feet so when I'm old I'll be able to walk a lot longer." I don't know how it'll turn out. But since sore feet cause pain, I was automatically against it. If I knew the pain was doing something good, however, I would feel different about it. It wouldn't be so bad.

We don't know what the future holds. It is always a possibility that the thing you hate so much right now is something you'll be happy for later. You don't know.

Therefore it is usually counterproductive to pass a negative judgment on *anything* that happens to you.

It is usually counterproductive for several reasons: First of all, you don't really know if it will turn out in your favor, so passing a negative judgment is putting confidence in an unprovable and possibly false guess. And that, of course, is not straight thinking.

Second, it puts you in a bad mood to pass a negative judgment like that and bad moods are bad for your health, bad for your relationships, and no fun.

Third, according to research at Cornell University, our minds find it easier to *confirm* a judgment than to *disconfirm* it. When you conclude something is bad, your judgment will alter the way you perceive your life in a way that confirms your conclusion.

The good news is, when you judge something as *good*, your mind works to confirm that judgment also. When you decide "maybe this is something good in disguise," you release the creativity of your brain to *find* ways it might be good — not only thinking of new ways to look at the situation, but thinking of ideas you can put into action that will *make* lemonade out of this lemon. When you conclude it's bad, you slam the door on those ways, and they become unavailable to you.

When something happens — anything — before you pass judgment, consider this: It may be good.

No matter what happens, consider the possibility that it may be good.

Nobody knows enough to
be a pessimist.

— *Norman Cousins*

You CAN Change

STANLEY SCHACHTER WAS PUZZLED. A researcher at Columbia University, Schachter was well-versed on the studies of weight-loss and smoking-cessation programs. According to the research, only 10 to 30 percent of the people who participate in those programs are still slender or nonsmoking one year later. Ten to 30 percent. That is a pretty bleak statistic.

These studies prompted some researchers and therapists to assert it's nearly impossible to stop smoking or control one's weight permanently. But this was a premature, overly-pessimistic conclusion, as you will see.

What puzzled Schachter was that *most* of the people he knew personally who wanted to lose weight or quit smoking seemed to have been able to do it successfully. He conducted interviews with his colleagues and friends, to find out if it was true, and the interviews confirmed his hunch: Those who had tried had succeeded. But how could the results of these interviews be reconciled with the studies showing such poor results from programs to quit smoking or lose weight?

Schachter spent over twenty years doing research on this, and he concluded that the key to success in changing long-standing habits is *practice.* This is an extremely important idea. According to his research, people who have successfully quit smoking have tried and *failed* a number of times before they finally succeeded. The same was true about losing weight. Apparently you have to *learn* how to *keep* the change, and after you learn how, it begins to become a new part of yourself that eventually requires very little active effort to maintain.

That's why the studies of weight-loss programs and stop-smoking studies look so bleak: Each is a study of only a *single* attempt. Schachter found that the more times you go through one of these programs, the more likely the change will be permanent.

So if you have tried to change and failed, try again. And *keep* trying. You *can* change...and you can learn how to keep the change. All you need is practice.

Keep persisting until the change you want happens.

A little more persistence, a little more effort, and what seemed hopeless failure may turn to glorious success.

— Elbert Hubbard

You may have a fresh start any moment you choose, for this thing we call "failure" is not the falling down, but the staying down.

— Mary Pickford

The Neutralizer

WHAT'S THE FIRST THING you do when you get a flat tire or when you burn your dinner or when one of your kids gets an F? When something goes wrong, you say something — to yourself or to someone else. If you're upset, you think or say *emotionally loaded* expressions, and those expressions — because they are emotionally loaded — intensify your upsetting feelings. Those expressions make things worse. They give you more bad feelings than is really necessary.

So when you find yourself thinking or saying a thought like "This is *terrible*," try changing it to a less emotional description — for example, "This is inconvenient." Notice how different the two statements are, emotionally speaking. Try saying each statement to yourself right now and check how different they feel.

It seems like a simple change to make, and it is. But it can change a setback from a *catastrophe* to merely annoying, at least in your experience.

The emotionally loaded comment doesn't help you. It may even hinder you from dealing with the situation rationally. The emotionally neutral statement "This is inconvenient," leads to an emotionally neutral response — in other words, a reasonable, practical response.

Try to become emotionally neutral when an emotionally charged response is counterproductive. Notice what you're thinking and try to make the same comment as a bland, computerlike description of the situation rather than a comment charged with emotion.

> Instead of "I *hate* her," say "What she did interfered with one of my goals."
>
> Rather than "Oh this is just great!" said with a bitter tone of voice, try something like "This isn't very good," said in an emotionless monotone.
>
> Change "#@*!#*#!!" to "I would have preferred it turned out differently."

WHEN YOU'RE SPEAKING to someone, your neutrality can help prevent the *other* person from getting upset and it'll keep your own emotional intensity to a minimum.

> Instead of complaining to your spouse "I am sick to death of car problems," try something like "Maybe it's time to get another car."
>
> Instead of yelling at your teenage son "I've had it up to *here* with you," how about saying this in an emotionally neutral tone of voice: "I've told you twice not to do that. Next time you do it, I will take away your TV for a week."

NEUTRALIZE THE NEGATIVE. It's a simple technique, but with practice it can level out some of the downturns in this roller-coaster ride we call life without in any way interfering with the upturns.

Describe upsetting situations to yourself in emotionally neutral words.

A Wiser Adviser

HAVE YOU EVER NOTICED how wise you are when you give advice to a person younger than you? You aren't fooling yourself. You really have gained some wisdom over the years. Have you ever wished you could be that wise when *you* had troubles? You can. You can talk to yourself like a "Dutch uncle."

Randall Masciana, M.S., tried to find out what kind of mental strategy would improve a person's performance when throwing darts. Masciana had the participants try everything from mental imagery to Zen. What worked best for improving the dart thrower's ability to hit the target was "positive self-talk."

Simply talking to yourself in a confident, reassuring, positive, friendly way makes a difference. It may be trite. It may be old. But it works, and it works better than anything else. The only catch is: It doesn't work unless you actually do it.

When things get tough, keep your thoughts prominent. Turn up the volume of your inner voice so you can hear it clearly, and coach yourself. If you don't know what to say, imagine a friend of yours or your little brother was in the same situation and say to yourself what you might say to him.

Another way of knowing what to say to yourself is to ask yourself what someone you admire would say to you: Abraham Lincoln, a favorite professor, your grandmother — whomever you admire for her or his wisdom and strength of character. Imagine asking the person for advice and imagine what s/he might say to you.

You know more about your own situation than anyone else, so your advice to yourself is in some ways more useful than anyone else's. You are wise. If you would only talk to yourself and listen, your life would be better.

Talk to yourself in a confident, reassuring, positive way.

Our lives are what our thoughts make them.

— Marcus Aurelius

People often say that motivation doesn't last. Well, neither does bathing — that's why we recommend it daily.

— Zig Ziglar

Stress Control

GETTING CRITICIZED by your supervisor; finding out someone you love has lied to you; receiving some bad news — these things cause stress. And stress has some negative consequences, as you probably know. But these are only stressful *events*. The source of stress that wreaks the greatest havoc on your health and sanity is *ongoing* stressful circumstances.

Like what? Like when a stepchild moves in with you, permanently disrupting the privacy you had with your spouse; or your younger brother marries someone who verbally abuses your favorite niece. These are the kinds of stresses you have to *live* with. They don't just come up and rock your world for a little while and then go away. They stay. And, like living in a house with a fire alarm going all day long, it starts to wear you down.

But there is something you can do about it. When you have an ongoing stressful circumstance in your life, you can modify your level of responsibility. Either take more responsibility or less. Start by asking yourself, "Am I trying to control something I can't or shouldn't control?" or "Is there something I should take responsibility for that I have been leaving out of my control?"

It would probably help to write it out rather than do it in your head. Write the questions and then jot down some ideas — where are you taking too much or too little control of some aspect of your life?

Be specific. You are responsible for your child in general, for example, but specifically, do you control what he wears or what he eats or when he goes to bed? *You* must decide. What exactly do you control and what is either out of your control or none of your business? *You* must decide.

If something is out of your control (or is none of your business and you've been trying to *make* it your business), you will relieve yourself of a lot of stress by letting go of it. Drop that one. Recognize it's out of your control and busy yourself with things that are in your control. You may be in the habit of trying to control that thing, so you'll have to remind yourself again and again for a couple weeks: "Oh yeah, I'm not trying to control that anymore." Write it on a card and carry it with you. Post notes to yourself on your bathroom mirror. Do whatever you have to do to remember you no longer have to waste your energy trying to control that thing.

Now, if you find something you should and can control and haven't been, roll up your sleeves and get to work on solving the problem. Use the problem-solving method on page 200. Deliberately take steps to repair the troubling circumstances. That'll relieve your stress better than anything else. It may be difficult at first; it may actually cause you *extra* stress to face the situation and try to deal with it, but in the long run, your stress level will go down.

Take responsibility for what you are responsible for, and stop taking responsibility for what is not your responsibility. It's that simple. Control what you *can* control, and let the rest go. It will relieve a great deal of your stress.

Control what is your responsibility.

The Old Switcheroo

WE ALL HAVE TIMES WHEN we think about something negative we can't do anything about: Something in the news, something that happened yesterday, one of our fellow workers who made us mad, a company policy. The time spent ruminating on that stuff is wasted. It's worse than wasted, because it makes our bodies produce stress hormones, which circulate in the bloodstream and aren't good for our health.

When you find yourself thinking about something negative and you want to stop, I'd like to give you a technique...but I can't. The mind doesn't work that way. It's like a river that just keeps flowing, and even when you try to dam it up, it just overflows the dam and keeps on flowing. A river must flow. You can't stop it.

But you can redirect it.

The same is true for your mind. It keeps flowing; it keeps thinking. You can't stop it. But you can redirect it.

When you are thinking about something negative you can't do anything about, redirect your mind. There are a million things you could direct your mind to, but let's choose a good one now rather than wait until we're bothered by something. Here's an extremely useful area to redirect your mind to: Complimenting other people.

You and I know we take things for granted and it would be good to appreciate what people do for us, but we don't, at least not as often as we'd like. Why? Because we need to think about it. When we compliment someone without giving it any thought, it comes out shallow, general, or phony. To do it well requires *thought.*

But we don't have the spare time to think about it — we're too busy thinking about negative things we can't do anything about (wink).

So from this point on, use the occurrence of needless negative rumination as a trigger — something that reminds you to think about complimenting someone. Use it as an opportunity to switch your mind, to turn it in a new direction. What specifically has someone done that you think was cool? Big or small, it doesn't matter. Next time you see that person, let them know you appreciate it. The fact that you acknowledge it some time after it happens shows it was important enough for you to think about later, which adds more impact to the compliment.

Give more sincere and well-thought-out compliments and your relationships will be better, your life will be better, the world will be better. And one way to give more compliments is to use the old switcheroo.

Direct your thoughts to what you appreciate and say it.

The measure of mental health is the disposition to find good everywhere.

— Ralph Waldo Emerson

Having the Time

I WAS JUST READING A TRUE STORY about a Norwegian soldier during World War Two who had been put out of action by frostbite and was confined to a small sled in the middle of the Arctic wilderness. Some friends were hiding him from the German soldiers who were occupying Norway. He was alone for twenty-seven days except for a short visit by someone about every three or four days. He had a book with him, but he didn't read much of it during those twenty-seven days. He "never seemed to have the time."

When I read that last line, it jolted me awake and has been bugging me ever since. Do you understand why? It was a ludicrous situation to be short of time in. Here was a man who couldn't walk, who was confined to a sleeping bag in the middle of a silent, snow-covered, completely uninhabited area in the Arctic, and he was too busy to read. What's wrong with this picture?

What's wrong is the same thing that's wrong with you and me. *We're too busy.* You are, aren't you? Yeah, so am I. Short of time. More things to do than you have time to do. Always trying to catch up.

But what has been dawning on me with a certain degree of irony and ridiculousness is that my lack of time is completely created by *me.*

There is no shortage of time. There is only the greedy effort to get more from our days than we can, while at the same time greedily wanting to also spend some of that time in leisure.

It's silly. And it's tragic. It costs us the experience of living. Time seems to fly by. Wow, where did those last two years go? Were we so busy getting things done we forgot to enjoy our own lives?

Let's just relax, shall we? Let's quit trying to do so much. We don't have to get *all* that stuff done. We don't have to be perfect parents — kids have been raised by imperfect parents for a long time and still turned out okay. We don't have to be perfect students. We don't have to be perfect at anything. We don't have to do it all. And we don't have to be happier. But when we realize we don't have to cram so much into our days, we will be.

If your own greed is making you discontent, quit cramming so much into your days.

Don't say you don't have enough time. You have exactly the same number of hours per day that were given to Helen Keller, Pasteur, Michelangelo, Mother Teresa, Leonardo da Vinci, Thomas Jefferson, and Albert Einstein.

— H. Jackson Brown

Think Positive Positively

WHEN A PERSON thinks a negative thought and tries to get rid of it, that person is thinking positively negatively. Daniel M. Wegner of Trinity University in San Antonio, Texas, has conducted a long string of experiments showing the futility and actual danger of trying to get rid of thoughts.

In some of the experiments, Wegner told his subjects, "Try not to think about a white bear." The subjects were then asked to say aloud everything that came to mind. Of course, thoughts of white bears showed up quite a bit. Trying *not* to think of a white bear produced a thought of a white bear between six and fifteen times in a five-minute period.

Trying not to think a negative thought will result in thinking it *more*.

Thinking is like breathing: It goes on night and day and you can't stop it. But you can *change* it. You can breathe slowly and deeply or shallowly and quickly. You can breathe any way you want. But you can't stop.

The same is true about thinking. You can say something stupid or depressing to yourself; you can say something intelligent or inspiring to yourself; but you can't stop saying something to yourself.

So when you find yourself disliking the contents of your thoughts, instead of trying to *stop* yourself from thinking a thought, try to *direct* your thoughts.

And one of the most powerful ways to direct your thinking is by asking yourself a question. A question gets your mind going in a new direction without suppressing what you're already thinking. Ask yourself a question.

Of course, the *kind* of question you ask makes a big difference. If you ask "Why is this happening to poor me?" your answers won't help you any.

The idea is to direct your mind by asking questions that put your attention on practical things, on accomplishment, on the future. If you find yourself worrying, for example, ask yourself something like this: "How can I make myself stronger and better able to deal with this?" Or "Can I get busy right now working on my goal — so busy I forget all about my worries? And if not, is there some planning I can do now that will save me time later?" Or even simply "What is my goal?"

When you find yourself thinking negatively about something "bad" that happened, ask yourself "What's *good* about this?" Or "How can I turn this to my advantage?" Or "What assumption have I made that I can argue with?" Ask a good question.

When you decide on a question to ask yourself, ask the question and *keep asking*. Ponder it. Wonder about it. Let it run through your mind whenever your mind isn't otherwise engaged. It will turn the tide of your thoughts and bring you into a new state of mind because you're thinking positively *positively*.

Direct your mind by asking yourself a good question.

Unpleasant Feelings

NEGATIVE FEELINGS PLAGUE all of us from time to time. Worry creeps into the mind like an unwelcome in-law, and if something isn't done about it, the worry will stay and eat you out of house and home. Anger strikes, pumping your body full of adrenaline, making it hard to concentrate on your work or speak with a civil tongue. Depression brings feelings of hopelessness and helplessness, darkening and saddening your world like a cold, bleak day in winter.

These are the three faces of negative feelings: Worry, anger, depression. Most negative feelings you ever feel are a shade of anxiety, anger, or sadness. You know these feelings are unpleasant. Hopefully you know they aren't good for your health. But what can you do to minimize the amount of time you feel them?

First, of course, is to look at the situation causing the negative feelings and change things if you can. But if there is nothing you can do about the situation, get involved in something that engages your mind and forget about it. Do not try to *stop* thinking negatively. Simply try to get absorbed in doing something constructive.

Purposeful activities occupy mind-space, and the more the task engages or takes up your attention, the more mind-space it occupies. Get involved enough in something or do something absorbing enough, and there's no more mind-space left to think about anything else.

What continues a negative emotion is *thinking* about it. Just as you can distract a crying child and he will forget his skinned knee, you can distract yourself with something so interesting or challenging or important, your mind will naturally stop thinking about the problem, and your negative feelings — now that you're no longer producing them with your thoughts — will dissipate.

Seek your escape from unnecessary negative feelings by *fleeing into a purpose.* It will take your mind off the negative thing, giving you a healthful break from those negative feelings. The side-effect is that something purposeful and productive gets done in the meantime. And that will give you something to feel *good* about.

Relieve negative feelings by turning your attention to purposeful activities.

This is the true joy in life, the being used for a purpose recognized by yourself as a mighty one; the being a force of nature instead of a feverish selfish clod of ailments and grievances complaining that the world will not devote itself to making you happy. I am of the opinion that my life belongs to the whole community and as long as I live it is my privilege to do for it whatever I can. I want to be thoroughly used up when I die, for the harder I work, the more I live. I rejoice in life for its own sake. Life is no "brief candle" to me. It is sort of a splendid torch which I have a hold of for the moment, and I want to make it burn as brightly as possible before handing it over to future generations.

— *George Bernard Shaw*

Pillar of Strength

IN HIS BOOK, *GRINDING IT OUT*, Ray Kroc, the man who made McDonald's what it is today, wrote about his father. Kroc senior was a hard-working man who was doing well in real estate before the Depression, expanding his holdings and using credit to extend himself even further. "When the market collapsed, he was crushed beneath a pile of deeds he could not sell," wrote Kroc. "The land they described was worth less than he owed. This was an unbearable situation for a man of my father's principled conservatism. He died of a cerebral hemorrhage in 1930. He had worried himself to death. On his desk the day he died were two pieces of paper — his last paycheck from the telegraph company and a garnishment notice for the entire amount of his wages."

Bad stuff happens, and sometimes it's big. You don't want it to crush you. You want to be strong. So start now taking every small bad thing that happens as an opportunity to repeat this idea to yourself:

> "There will be an advantage in this. I will find it or I will make it."

Repeat it until you *see* or can *make* an advantage out of it. If you will do this, you will stand as a fortress of strength for your family in situations that would make lesser men and women collapse in hopelessness.

This idea is not some namby-pamby, rah-rah, positive-thinking nonsense. It is a source of tremendous strength. It may save your life some day. For sure it will be good for your health. Ingrain that thought — make that pathway through your brain well-worn — and you'll be able to face up to difficulties that would make a mere mortal crawl and whimper.

Arnold Schwarzenegger is more successful than most people know. He's made a lot of money with his films and married a Kennedy, but he's also a smart and successful businessman outside of the movie business, with real estate, books, restaurants, and fitness clubs. He is hugely successful. (Editor's update: This was originally written in 1998, and by now Schwarzenegger has been the governor of California.) In his autobiography, he wrote,

> "I didn't get certain things I needed as a child, and that, I think, finally made me hungry for achievement...If I'd gotten everything and been well-balanced, I wouldn't have had my drive. [Because of] this negative element in my upbringing, I had a positive drive toward success..."

He held up under the strain and turned it to his advantage. He didn't let it crush him because of the way he thinks. This strength is within your grasp: Find or make an advantage out of everything that happens.

Find a way to turn your problems into an advantage.

Solitude and Time

MOST PEOPLE HAVE A HEALTHY craving for quiet solitude. I know a few are afraid of being alone, but the rest of us find it soothing and rejuvenating and it doesn't happen nearly as much as we'd like.

Solitude is therapeutic. Spending time in solitude doing what you want at a pace that is natural to you, without any interruptions, without having to take others into consideration, without the need to hurry, is deeply satisfying and personally I classify it as a psychological *need.*

It is *unnatural* for human beings to have no time to think. Time spent alone serves an important function, much in the same way dreaming does.

Dreaming may seem to be a waste of time, but when people are prevented from dreaming — allowed to sleep as much as they want but awakened when they start to dream — after a short while, they begin to hallucinate while they're awake. Dreaming is necessary for mental health.

I believe time to think is necessary too. If you prevent yourself from having time to do nothing, by yourself, allowing free time to think naturally, it makes you less calm, less rational, less happy, and less sane than you otherwise would be.

In solitude, in the absence of interruptions and distractions, the mind naturally drifts to solving problems, trying out solutions, imagining conversations, and figuring things out.

Of course, too much time alone isn't healthy either. It's like anything else, you need balance. Not enough exercise is unhealthy, but too much exercise could potentially put you in the hospital.

But most of us are deficient in solitude and need *more* of it. Finding the time and taking advantage of it may require some ingenuity on your part. But you can probably find a way, and you'll be glad you did.

Get enough time alone.

These are the voices which we hear in solitude, but they grow faint and inaudible as we enter into the world.

— Ralph Waldo Emerson

The great omission in American life is solitude...that zone of time and space, free from the outside pressures, which is the incinerator of the spirit.

— Marya Mannes

Meanings and Feelings

STANLEY SCHACHTER SET UP the following experiment: He first divided his experimental subjects into two groups and gave them all a shot of adrenaline (without telling them what it was). Then the subjects mingled with Schachter's assistants, whom the subjects had been led to believe were given a shot of the same substance.

In one group, the assistants acted as if they were experiencing anxiety. In the other group, the assistants acted excited and happy. Asked what the shot had done to them, subjects in the first group said the adrenaline shot made them feel anxious; subjects in the second group said the adrenaline made them feel excited and elated.

The way the assistants acted influenced the way the subjects interpreted their experience. And it was those *interpretations* that made their experience pleasant or unpleasant.

The adrenaline shot was the same in both groups, and caused the same effects: it made their hearts pound, dilated their eyes, sent glucose to the muscles, and shut down the digestive tract.

Both groups experienced the same *physical* changes, but the way the assistants *acted* created a different meaning for the physical changes, and those meanings made the difference between anxiety and elation.

Change the meaning of an experience and the experience changes. Please remember that. When the meaning changes, the experience changes. And you can change the meaning of an event deliberately.

The late Viktor Frankl, a psychiatrist and a survivor of Hitler's concentration camps, often changed the meaning of events for his patients, and it changed their lives. For example, an elderly and severely depressed man came to see Frankl. His wife had died and she had meant more to him than anything in the world.

"What would have happened," Frankl asked the man, "if you had died first, and your wife would have survived you?"

The man answered: "Oh, for her this would have been terrible; how she would have suffered!"

"You see," said Frankl, "such a suffering has been spared her, and it is you who have spared her this suffering; but now, you have to pay for it by surviving and mourning her."

The man didn't say anything. He shook Dr. Frankl's hand and calmly left. Frankl wrote:

> "Suffering ceases to be suffering in some way at the moment it finds a meaning, such as the meaning of a sacrifice."

The meanings you make in your life can be the difference between anxiety and elation, between hopelessness and courage, between failure and success, and even, as Frankl discovered in the concentration camps, between living and dying.

You have some control over the way you interpret the events of your life. The meanings of events are not written in stone. You can create more useful meanings for yourself. All it takes is a little thought.

Interpret events in a way that helps you.

Expect the Best

NOELLE CAME TO WORK worried about her roommate, Jana, who didn't come home the night before and didn't call. That wasn't like Jana, and Noelle was worried.

But Noelle's worry did not benefit Jana, and it harmed Noelle. Worry put stress hormones into her bloodstream, which isn't healthy. It suppressed her immune system. If she worries a lot, it will damage the inside of her arteries, which can end in a heart attack or stroke many years in the future. If she worries a lot, the stress hormones will actually destroy brain cells! Needless worry is a cost without a benefit. And it's not pleasant.

If you are worrying and want to stop, first ask yourself if there's anything you're going to do about the situation. If not, then start wondering what *good* things might be happening. Do not try to stop worrying.

Research by Daniel Wegner, PhD, of the University of Virginia has repeatedly shown that *trying to suppress thoughts* only results in thinking those thoughts more. If you try to suppress a thought hard enough, that thought can become an obsession.

I can't emphasize this enough, because although you are reading this and understand it, three weeks from now, you will probably try *not* to worry or try *not* to think a negative thought or try *not* to feel a negative emotion. It does not work. Please try to remember this.

If you try to stop worrying, you'll worry even more. What you want to do is give your mind a bone to chew on, but a different bone.

Worrying is imagining something bad happening. So simply imagine something *good* happening, and there will be less room in your mind for imagining something bad happening. Your mind has its limits, like the RAM of a computer. Give it enough to do, and it won't have enough free space to do anything else.

If worrying is a habit for you, it won't go away immediately. Every time you start to worry, ask yourself what good might be happening. And keep asking and wondering *and then leave it at that* — an open-ended possibility. Do this and something good will be happening to *you*: You will feel better and you'll be healthier.

By the way, Jana had a wonderful time.

Wonder about what good things might be happening.

Worry is a dark room where fears are developed and enlarged.

— Teresa Eagel

Blind Spots

COVER YOUR LEFT EYE, hold this page close to you, and look at the X. As you slowly pull the book away from you, at some point the 0 will disappear. Or cover your right eye and look at the 0, and pull the book away, and the X will disappear.

X 0

You have a blind spot in each eye where the bundles of nerve fibers go back into your brain. But notice something: *You don't see the blind spot.* It doesn't show up like a dark, empty spot. Your brain fills in the emptiness.

In a similar way, when there is information you don't know, your brain fills it in, giving you the feeling that nothing is missing.

In other words, when you feel certain, it doesn't really mean much. Your feeling of certainty doesn't necessarily have any relationship to your actual correctness or knowledge. Your brain produces a feeling of certainty at the drop of a hat because it's wired up to do so.

All human brains tend to jump to conclusions and then feel certain about those conclusions, so it pays to be somewhat skeptical of your own mind. That may seem like a negative goal, but it isn't. Feeling certain has caused more problems for people than skepticism ever did. For example, when you're arguing with someone, the thing that keeps the anger intense is that you're both certain you're right. If each of you had a little more skepticism about your own ability to remember and reason, it would be easier to work out your differences.

To take another example, depressed people would get depressed less often or less deeply if they became more skeptical of the pessimistic assumptions they are making. The feeling of certainty depressed people have about their own pessimistic view of the world does them harm.

Don't place much importance in your feelings of certainty. Be skeptical. Recognize you have blind spots and act accordingly. You'll be saner if you do.

Be skeptical of your feelings of certainty.

Well, I think we tried very hard not to be overconfident, because when you get overconfident, that's when something snaps up and bites you.

— Neil Armstrong

End of the World

EDNA FOA CONDUCTED research on social anxiety to find out what reduced anxiety the most. She discovered that what worked best was changing the way a person thought about *consequences.* That was the key to whether someone succeeded or failed to reduce his anxiety.

Specifically, anxious people expect the consequences of negative events to be worse than they would actually be. And of course this makes them more anxious then they need to be.

When you worry about something, you're asking yourself, "What if?" You wonder, *What if X happened?* And you think the consequences would be terrible. That's what scares you. What most worriers do is stop right there. They don't think beyond it. They wonder, "What if that happened?" and it scares them so much they don't want to think any more about it. But when you make yourself follow through on the question, your anxiety is usually cured in short order. Let me give you an example.

When my wife and I first got married, whenever we had an argument, it made me very upset. I was always afraid the argument would bring our relationship to an end. My question was, "What if we get divorced?" It sounds stupid now, but I never once thought beyond that. It was too awful to contemplate. This is my best friend. This is the one I love with all my heart. It was too terrifying to think any further than divorce. This worry put me in a panic, and my desperation only made those arguments worse.

When it got too heated, she (sensibly) wanted to leave and go for a walk or at least go into the other room. I wouldn't let her go until we had resolved our argument. Of course, it is almost impossible to resolve an argument between two people when both are upset, so my actions prolonged our arguments tremendously.

One day I asked her how she managed to stay so calm when we argued. I always seemed to flip out but even when she was mad, she never got anxious or desperate.

"Do any thoughts go through your mind when we're arguing?" I asked, "Do you say anything to yourself? Do you picture something?"

Turns out, she did something very specific. She did it every time and it kept her calm. Like me, she also had the thought, "What if this is the end of us?" But she didn't stop there. She deliberately imagined the worst that could happen. She tried to see a little movie in her mind of what would happen if we *did* divorce. She imagined going through the sadness, moving to a different place, and going on with her life.

And as she imagined time passing, she could see that she would survive, and even if this tragic thing happened, there would actually be some happiness down the road.

This seemed like a pretty straightforward technique, so I gave it a try and it really calmed me down. Our fights became less intense because I wasn't trying so hard to end the upset.

Imagining the worst produced two helpful results: First, imagining us moving away from each other always makes me sad. No matter how angry I am when I start thinking about it, I always feel sad because I realize how much I would miss her. That is a good realization to have during a fight.

The second benefit was realizing that even if that worst-case-scenario happened, I could still go on and eventually be happy. That helps me keep the situation in perspective and helps me calm down. And my lower anxiety helps me listen and speak more calmly.

I tried it the very next time we had an argument. It worked beautifully. It may have been the first time we ever argued that I stayed relatively calm. I didn't panic at all. I didn't get desperate. I tried it again the next argument. And the next. And that's about all it took. That was twenty-eight years ago, and now I never even consider the possibility that an argument spells doom. It totally cured me of that particular anxiety.

All I did was think beyond the original fear. Try it with one of your fears right now. You're afraid of what? Okay, what if it happened? Really, think about it. What if that terrible thing actually happened? What would come next? And *then* what? And *then* what?

Jim says, "I get nervous at work because I'm afraid my boss is going to get mad at me."

I say, "Okay, what if he does?"

Jim: "It would be upsetting."

Me: "Yeah, so? Then what would happen?"

Jim: "He might write me up. That means it would be a warning, and one more and I'll be fired!"

Me: "Okay, let's say that happens. He writes you up, you don't improve, and then he fires you. Then what would you do?"

Jim: "I'd have to find another job."

Me: "Okay. Could you do that?"

Jim: "Yeah, I think so, but it might not pay as much as I'm making now."

Me: "So? What would you do then?"

Jim: "I'd have to buy fewer things."

When you follow the line of questioning, it always seems to peter out into something that is not very catastrophic. You realize you could handle it. You'd live. It may be difficult. It may be a challenge, but it is nothing to get too distraught over.

According to the research, the two biggest mistakes anxious people tend to make is that they think an undesirable possibility is *more likely* than it really is, and they think if the bad thing happened, the consequences would be *more horrible* than they really would be.

This is the antidote: Ask the question, "What would happen then?" and keep following the consequences out to their natural conclusion.

I need to warn you: It won't work to tell yourself, "It'll be okay." That kind of shortcut doesn't have any impact on anxiety. You must go through the visualization. *See it happening* and see how you'd handle it. Be honest in your imaginings. Try to make it true-to-life. Don't try to imagine it more positively than you really think would happen. What do you think would *really* happen? Imagine it. Take a hard and honest look at it. And what do you think you'd *really* do about it? This will have a definite — and maybe even a dramatic — effect on your feelings.

Like a magic bullet, it goes to the heart of your worry and dissolves it.

In his book, *How to Stop Worrying and Start Living*, Dale Carnegie tells the story of a man who cured himself of a very serious case of anxiety using a method very similar to this. His name was Earl Haney and he had ulcers. Bad ulcers. One night he had a hemorrhage and was rushed to a hospital. He had holes in his stomach lining and had to have his stomach pumped every day. His diet was alkaline powder and tablespoon of half-and-half per hour. That's it. He was in bad shape.

This continued for *several months*. His weight dropped from 175 pounds to 90 pounds. Three doctors agreed he was terminal. Death was inevitable.

Suddenly a thought dawned on Earl. He realized he always wanted to travel the world before he died and he figured if he was going to do it, he'd better go now. Of course, his doctors were against it. Earl would have to pump his own stomach twice a day. Crazy!

Earl went ahead with his plans anyway. He bought a casket and took it with him so if he died on the trip, he could be buried in the family plot back home. He boarded a ship from Los Angeles to visit China and India. During the voyage, he gradually gave up all the pampering and stomach pumping. He let it go. If he was going to die, so be it. He started eating whatever he wanted. His worry and tension evaporated.

Even during a typhoon, which should have scared him to death, he actually enjoyed it because he had already looked at the consequences: He would die and his body would be sent back to Nebraska. His alternative was wasting away in a hospital, and he'd much rather die in a typhoon on his way to China.

He started really enjoying himself (now that he was free of constant worries) and he gained 90 pounds on the trip. His health returned. When he got home, he went back to work and said he never felt better in his life.

You can recover from your *own* worries. Go through the process, not trying to be positive, but being *realistic*. What you will discover is that the thing you fear so much might not be the calamity you made it out to be. And your increased calm will help make a calamity even *less* likely.

Imagine the worst that could happen and really look at it honestly.

How to Improve Your Self-Esteem

SELF-ESTEEM IS SELF-WORTH or self-value. So to increase your self-esteem, increase your worth or value. A lot of people would interpret that to mean "change the way you *think* about your worth or value." But I mean change what you do in order to make yourself worth more — to yourself and others. Make yourself worth more *in reality*, not just in your mind.

How? Here are four ways to go about it:

1. Gain more ability. If you are a manager, you could take classes or read books to increase your ability to manage. If you live in fear of physical harm, you could take a self-defense class. Become more able to do what needs to be done.

2. Become more honest. Every person has been dishonest. And you know it feels bad. It doesn't make you feel good about yourself, does it? And that's why every effort you make to become even a little more honest will make you worth more to yourself, and so improve your self-esteem. It will increase your personal pride in a healthy way. You will esteem yourself more highly.

3. Do something worthwhile. Are you doing something worthwhile? That depends on what I mean by "worthwhile," doesn't it? No! It depends on what *you* consider worthwhile. In order to feel self-worth, you need to know you're doing something *worthwhile*. Otherwise, your self-worth would be a sham. So spend some time wondering what that worthwhile task might be for you. It is a worthwhile pursuit to find a worthwhile pursuit! Check out the chapter in this book, *I Don't Know What To Do With My Life*, to find some ideas on how to find a worthwhile pursuit.

4. Acknowledge people. Try to give three good acknowledgments a day. It's a whole new way of life. This isn't nearly as easy and superficial as you might think at first. And it will increase your self-esteem.

All four of these things improve your value and worth, to yourself and other people. And that's what self-esteem is all about.

To increase your own self-esteem:
Gain more ability, become more honest, do something worthwhile, and acknowledge people.

We see things not as they are,
but as we are.

— H.M. Tomlinson

All in Your Head

IN 1914, A SMALL SHIP SAILED into the icy Weddell Sea, on its way to the South Pole. It carried a crew of twenty-seven men, and their leader, Ernest Shackleton. But unseasonable gales shoved the floating ice together and the temperature sank below zero, freezing more than a million square miles of ice into a solid mass. And they were stuck in the middle of it. They had no radio transmitter. They were alone.

For ten months the pressure increased until it crushed the ship, stranding them in the middle of an icy wasteland which could, at any time, break up and become a sea of floating ice chunks. They had to get off this ice while it was still solid, so they headed for the nearest known land, 346 miles away, dragging their two lifeboats over the ice.

But every few hundred yards they ran into a pressure ridge, sometimes two stories high, caused by the ice compacting. They had to chop through it.

At the end of two backbreaking days in subzero weather, they were exhausted. After all their hacking and dragging, they had traveled only two miles.

They tried again. In five days they went a total of nine miles, but the ice was becoming softer and the pressure ridges were becoming larger. They could go no further. So they had to wait...for several months.

Finally the ice opened up and they launched the boats into the churning mass of giant chunks of ice and barely made it to the open ocean in one piece. But now they were sailing across a treacherous sea. They landed on a tiny, barren, ice-covered, lifeless island in the middle of nowhere.

To save themselves, they needed to reach the nearest outpost of civilization: South Georgia, 870 miles away! Shackleton and five men took the best lifeboat and sailed across the Drake Passage, the most formidable piece of ocean in the world. Gales blow nonstop — up to 200 miles an hour (that's as hard as a hurricane) — and waves get as high as ninety feet. Their chances of making it were very close to zero.

But determination can change the odds.

They made it. But they landed on the wrong side of the island, and their boat was pounded into the rocks and rendered useless. The whaling port they needed to reach was on the *other* side of the island, which has mountain peaks 10,000 feet high and had never been crossed before.

They were the first. They didn't have much choice.

When they staggered into the little whaling port on the other side of the island, everyone who saw them stopped dead in their tracks. The three men had coal-black skin from the seal oil they had been burning as fuel. They had long, black dreadlocks. Their clothing was shredded, filthy rags, and they had come from the direction of the *mountains*. Nobody in the history of the whaling port had ever been known to enter the town from that direction.

Although all the men at that whaling port had known about Shackleton's expedition, his ship had been gone for seventeen months and was assumed to have sunk, and the crew with it. The whalers knew how deadly and unforgiving the ice could be.

The three ragged men made their way to the home of a man Shackleton knew, followed in silence by a growing crowd of people. When the man came to the door, he stepped back and stared in silence. Then he said, "Who the hell are you?"

The man in the center took a step forward and said, "My name is Shackleton."

According to some witnesses, the hard-faced man at the door turned away and wept.

This story is incredible, and if it weren't for the extensive verification and corroboration of the diaries and interviews with the men on the crew in Alfred Lansing's account, *Endurance*, it might easily be disbelieved. The story is true, and as incredible as what I've told you seems, I've only given you some highlights.

After many attempts to get through the ice, on August 30th — almost two years since they had embarked — Shackleton made it back to that barren island and rescued the rest of his men. Every man in Shackleton's crew made it home alive.

Fifteen years earlier, a different ship got stuck in the ice in the Weddell Sea — the *Belgica*, led by Adrien de Gerlache — but they didn't do so well. During the winter in the Antarctic, the sun completely disappears below the horizon for seventy-nine days. Shackleton's crew endured it. But the crew of the *Belgica* grew depressed, gave up hope, and succumbed to negative thinking. Some of them couldn't eat. Mental illness took over. One man had a heart attack from a terror of darkness. Paranoia and hysteria ran rampant.

None of this happened to Shackleton's men because he insisted they keep a good attitude, and he did the same. He once said that the most important quality for an explorer was *not* courage or patience, but *optimism*. He said, "Optimism nullifies disappointment and makes one more ready than ever to go on."

Shackleton also knew that attitudes are contagious. He was fully aware of the fact that if anyone lost hope they wouldn't be able to put forth that last ounce of energy which may make the difference. And they *did* get pushed to the limits of human endurance. But he had convinced himself and his men they would make it out alive. His determination to remain optimistic ultimately saved their lives.

And it can achieve great things for you too. It comes down to what you say: Either *you* say it's hopeless or *you* say it can be done. You can never look into the future to find the answer. It's in your head.

Make up your mind you will succeed.

Every noble work is, at first, impossible.

— Thomas Carlyle

History has demonstrated that the most notable winners usually encountered heartbreaking obstacles before they triumphed. They won because they refused to become discouraged by their defeats.

— B.C. Forbes

Think Strong

SOME PEOPLE ARE EMOTIONALLY stronger than others. They can take a lot of stress and strain without falling apart, while others collapse into a whimpering heap at the smallest things.

One of the most important differences between an emotionally weak person and an emotionally strong person is *what they think* when things go wrong. When troubles come along, a weak person is in the habit of thinking things like this: "This is more than I can stand." A tough one thinks something more like: "I can handle this."

It doesn't matter what specific words a person puts to the two different kinds of thinking. The general principle is that the kind of thoughts that make people weak are feeble and impotent: "I can't take it, it's too overwhelming, it's too much to bear, I can't stand it, I'm not up to this, I'm not emotionally ready for this," etc.

The thoughts that make you strong are capable and resolute: "I can take it, everything is going to work out, I'll get through it, maybe there's a lesson in it for me, adversity builds character, I'm tough, people have been through worse, if I try I can find an advantage in all this, when it's over I'll be wiser," etc.

To become stronger, *change your thoughts*. It's as simple and uncomplicated as that. There's nothing to it but to do it.

Start saying something different to yourself during tough times. When you feel stress, coach yourself, "Come on, [your name here], you can handle this. When this is over, you might even be a stronger person because of it."

Think strong thoughts and you will be tougher, braver, and more resilient. Just like that.

The stronger thoughts are *truer* than the weaker thoughts. You *can* take it. Human beings, including you, can withstand a tremendous amount of strain without cracking, as any cursory perusal of war stories, survival accounts, and reports of disasters demonstrate.

These kinds of thoughts won't be habitual at first, of course. The way you think is as much a habit as the way you tie your shoes. But keep deliberately thinking stronger, and after awhile it will *become* habitual. Eventually, you'll wonder how you ever thought differently.

Would you like to be stronger? Would you like to have more emotional calm during the stressful times? Would you like to stand as a pillar of strength when those about you are crumbling? Sure you would. This is the way. Change your thoughts. Make them stronger. Don't think you can do it? That's the *first* thought to change.

Think thoughts that give you strength and make you tough.

Happy, satisfied persons control their mental attitude. They take a positive view of their situation. They look for the good, and when something isn't so good, they look first to themselves to see if they can improve it.

— Napoleon Hill and W. Clement Stone

Where to Tap

EVER HEAR THE STORY of the giant ship engine that failed? The ship's owners tried one expert after another, but none of them could figure out how to fix the engine. Then they hired an old man who had been fixing ships since he was a kid. He carried a large bag of tools with him, and when he arrived, he immediately went to work. He inspected the engine carefully, top to bottom. Two of the ship's owners were there, watching this man, hoping he would know what to do. After looking things over, the old man reached into his bag and pulled out a small hammer. He gently tapped something. *Instantly*, the engine lurched into life. It was fixed!

A week later, the owners received a bill from the old man for ten thousand dollars.

"What?!" the owners exclaimed. "He hardly did anything!" So they wrote the old man a note saying, "Please send us an itemized bill."

The man sent a bill that read,

Tapping with a hammer: $2.00
Knowing where to tap: $9998.00

Effort is important, but knowing *where* to make an effort in your life makes all the difference. And here's something I've learned from experience and study: If you want to improve your life overall, the best place to tap is *exercise*. It will give you the most benefits for the least amount of time put into it.

I injured a tendon not too long ago and didn't exercise for about a month. During that month, I didn't really notice the loss of anything. But I've started again, and I've become a born-again exerciser! I'd forgotten how good it is for my sense of well-being. I have more energy, a better attitude, a gentler disposition. It's easier to be the kind of person I want to be.

Our bodies *need* exercise. It isn't a *bonus*, it's a *necessity*. And when we don't exercise, it makes us feel bad. We may not even notice we feel bad until we compare it to how it feels when we start exercising. It's our natural state to be energetic and feeling good. But the lack of exercise prevents us from feeling that way. Exercise is not *optional*. If you want to feel good often, it is *essential*.

A consensus is building among doctors, psychologists and those trying to help others become saner, happier and healthier: Exercise is the place to start. If you were in a position to give advice, and someone unhappy or unhealthy came to you for guidance but you were allowed to give only one word of advice, the best thing you could recommend is: Exercise!

Exercise regularly.

Following 32,000 people for eight years, [Steven Blair] found that those whose only risk [factor] was inactivity were more likely to die prematurely than those who had high cholesterol, high blood pressure, and a smoking habit but who got some exercise each day.

— *Katherine Griffin*

A Simple Way to Change How You Feel

SOMETIMES WHEN YOU WANT to behave differently, you don't feel like it when the time comes. And sometimes when you want to feel differently, you don't really know how to get there from where you are. Maybe you want to feel confident talking with strangers or feel cheerful at work, but you don't know *how* to feel confident or cheerful. Well, there is a way.

The principle is simple: Assume the *posture* you would have if you felt the way you *want* to feel, *breathe* the way you would breathe, talk the way you would talk, think the things you would think, act the way you would act — do the things you would do if you felt the way you want to feel.

Are you depressed and want to feel happy? Move your body like you move it when you're happy. If you can't remember what it's like to be happy, move your body the same way you've seen *others* move when *they* looked happy. Put the same expression on your face. Imagine or remember the way you talk to yourself and the kind of perspective you might have about your situation when you're happy, and then say those things to yourself and take that perspective.

In other words, *act as though* you were happy.

If you are angry and want to be calm, act as though you were calm. Do you feel weak and want to be strong? Act as though you were strong.

What you're doing is changing everything that *can* be changed, and this changes your feelings, which can't be changed directly.

Remember Pavlov's dogs? Pavlov rang a bell every time he fed the dogs, and the dogs associated the sound of the bell with the taste of food. So when the bell rang, the dogs salivated, even when there was no food.

For your whole life you've been relating certain body postures, facial expressions, breathing patterns, etc., to certain feelings like happiness or calmness or strength. The postures and facial expressions and feelings belong together. So when you act as though you're relaxed, you begin to feel relaxed. When you act as though you feel good, you begin to feel good. And after awhile, you aren't acting. It's like siphoning gas — you have to suck on the hose at first, but then it comes out by itself.

"Acting as though" also *changes reality*, which tends to reinforce the feelings. For example, people who feel depressed typically aren't very friendly. If they acted like a person who felt good, they would act friendlier, and most people would respond by being friendly in return, which would make the person *feel less depressed*. It creates an upward spiral.

Most people forget about changing their posture, their thoughts, and their breathing, so *start* with those. *Then* add changing the way you talk, the expression on your face, the way you move, etc. It works better that way.

Change how you act and what you do and your feelings will change. You'll get a better response from the world, which will reinforce your good feelings.

Act as though you already feel the way you want to feel.

We've Been Duped

PEOPLE FELT RICHER in the 1950s — when houses averaged 1100 square feet — than they do now, when they average 2000 square feet. There were no DVDs, no microwaves, no cable TV, no iPhones, no video games, hardly any dishwashers, and in most homes only the father brought in an income. Yet according to surveys, our reported level of happiness peaked in 1957 and has gone down as our level of wealth has gone up.

The reason is simple: You and I don't need much to be happy. Most of us are doing too much, working too hard, trying to make "enough" money. But it costs us time. And after a certain point — a point most of us have passed a long time ago — you get less and less happiness for more and more expenditure of time to earn money. And that is time taken away from time spent with your loved ones, where a good deal of happiness *does* come from. Those moments of simple human interaction — talking, playing a game, taking a walk, cooking together — those are the real riches of life.

You have been exposed to a barrage of advertising, something like a million ads by the time you're twenty. And those advertising people are *experts* on human nature. They've carefully read the studies showing what influences people, and they design their advertisements to pull your attention and convince you their product would make you happy. They have been trying to manipulate your values since you were a kid. They've been trying to get you to believe *having* things is what will make you happy.

Most of us are way too busy, and that's just perfect as far as the advertisers are concerned. We're out working to earn more money so we have more to spend on products. If we would learn to curb our desire for so much stuff, we wouldn't have to work as much, so we'd be able to spend more unscheduled time with our loved ones.

You already know this, I'm sure. But the more you hear something the more of an impact it will make on your feelings and behavior. Ask any advertiser.

You want more *time?* You want more *enjoyment?* There is a way, but it will require a little discipline: Do without. You'll be a lot richer.

Remind yourself you don't need much to be happy.

Wealth consists not in having great possessions, but in having few wants.

— Epictetus

Every day is a bank account, and time is our currency. No one is rich, no one is poor, we've got 24 hours each.

— Christopher Rice

How to Like Yourself More

IT'S IMPOSSIBLE TO LIKE YOURSELF much when you're doing something you think is wrong. It doesn't matter how much rationalization you do, or how thickly you try to cover it with justification, if you think it's wrong or bad, and you keep doing it, you cannot like yourself.

So the way to like yourself more is to clean up your integrity. You may not like to hear that, and I don't blame you. It sounds like a horrible burden. But it's not. It lightens your load and makes it more fun to be alive. Here are three steps to a self you like and respect.

1. Make a list of what you're doing that you think is wrong and stop doing those things. You might keep backsliding for awhile, but if you keep at it, you'll make it. Also make a list of things you *should* be doing and aren't. Never mind what others think you should or shouldn't do or what you've been told is right or wrong. Just pay attention to what *you* feel is right or wrong. And make sure you write it out. This, by itself, will give you some relief, because we are never as bad as we think we are. When you write it out, you'll see that. The list will be *finite*. Work on one thing at a time. Then cross it off your list.

2. Make amends for anything you've done in the past that you feel guilty about. Some situations only need an apology, or just an admission that you did it. Other situations will require you to

take some action to make up for the damage you did. Before you get started on this, you should know that it's never as bad as you think it will be. It's easier to make amends than it first may seem. Be creative. Make it fun. You may come up with a wild idea, but if it seems right to you, try it.

3. Forgive yourself for all the "bad" things you've done. This should be fairly easy since you have already taken responsibility for your past and present action. But to finish the job, you need to forgive yourself. To forgive yourself simply means to give up resentment against yourself, or give up the desire to punish yourself. Since you've taken and are taking responsibility for your actions, to continue to punish yourself or resent yourself is just silly. You are human. Humans make mistakes. You have recognized that and corrected your mistakes. That's something to feel *good* about. So forgive yourself. A decision is all that's required. Simply decide to stop resenting yourself and give up any intentions of punishing yourself.

TAKE THESE THREE steps to a self you really like. You'll gain strength and confidence and the peace that comes from knowing you do what's right.

Clean up your integrity.

If You Relapse

A THERAPIST ONCE TOLD ME he had a client — we'll call him Dirck — who's wife didn't feel loved. The therapist helped Dirck find out what his wife needed to feel loved. She craved physical demonstration: Hugs, touches, kisses, holding hands. These really got through to her and meant the most to her. Dirck had been simply *telling* her how much he loved her without doing much physical demonstration. For some people that would have been just great, but not for Dirck's wife. She heard the words but it didn't have the emotional impact she wanted. Although she knew *intellectually* Dirck loved her, she didn't *feel* loved.

The therapist helped Dirck learn to demonstrate his love physically. Dirck returned a week later to say, "It worked! She feels loved and we are both very happy."

Six months later, Dirck was back. His wife didn't feel loved any more. The therapy apparently hadn't succeeded like he thought.

With a few simple questions, the therapist found out Dirck had stopped doing what he was doing before and was merely professing his love with words again!

As stupid as that sounds, you will have to be careful to avoid making the same mistake. When things are going well, you will tend to take your attention off the problem, which is good. But if you stop taking the *actions* that made things go fine, your progress will be undone, and one day you'll realize you've relapsed, and you may even throw up your hands in despair because "apparently this stuff doesn't work as well as I thought it did."

Knowledge isn't enough. You have to *take the steps* if you want to reap the benefits. The only thing that makes this difficult is: It's hard to notice the *absence* of a negative condition (except immediately after it goes away). That's just a fact of life. When things go wrong, you *really* notice it. When things go fine, you don't really notice. That's just the way the human brain works.

And the ultimate outcome of not noticing the absence of negative conditions is relapsing or backsliding. But it isn't really a big deal. Just remember what works. And when you notice you've relapsed, start doing *again* what worked *before*.

When you relapse, go back to doing what works.

Part of recovery is relapse. I dust myself off and move forward again.

— Steven Adler

Rather than viewing a brief relapse back to inactivity as a failure, treat it as a challenge and try to get back on track as soon as possible.

— Jimmy Connors

Rx to Relax

WHEN YOU GET ANGRY, upset, anxious, tense, frustrated or worried, adrenaline goes into your blood stream. It makes your heart beat faster, putting strain on your cardiovascular system. These strains add up, and later in life, things can go wrong because of it. Every time you are able to lessen the intensity of one of these feelings, it will benefit your health. It also makes your life a more pleasant experience.

There is a very simple way to lower your adrenaline level: Relax. Here's how to relax on the spot:

1. Breathe deeply. When you tense up, your breathing gets quicker, shallower, and higher in the chest. You'll feel better right away (and your heart will slow down) if you'll just make your breathing more relaxed. Deeper. Slower. Sigh in a relaxed way. A slow out-breath is more important than a slow in-breath.

2. Loosen tensed muscles. Just about any time, but especially when you've got the adrenaline pumping, muscles tend to tighten, particularly muscles around your neck, upper back, and face. Pay attention to your muscles in those areas and when you find one that's contracting for no good reason, relax it. If at first you have trouble relaxing a muscle, tense it first, then relax it.

3. Say the word "relax" to yourself. Make sure your inner voice is relaxing. Don't yell at yourself, "Relax!!" Say it soothingly.

These three tasks are easy to do, can be done in the midst of your work, and will slow your heart down to a healthier level. When you become more relaxed, you think better, you're more creative, and you can use more of what you know — including what you know about human relations, so you'll get along with people better. Your life will be smoother. Try it and see for yourself.

**Breathe deeply, loosen tensed muscles,
and say to yourself, "Relax."**

---

*Stress is an ignorant state. It believes that
everything is an emergency.*

— Natalie Goldberg

*A crust eaten in peace is better than a banquet
partaken in anxiety.*

— Aesop

Interest is Life

PEOPLE WHO ARE FULLY VITAL and alive and full of energy are *interested.* They're pursuing an interest. The stronger the interest, the more vitality emanates from it. People without any interests at all are bored, tired and lifeless. Interest is everything.

Here's the problem: You can't fake it or force yourself to be interested in something. You can gently open yourself to be mildly interested, but you're either strongly interested in something or you are not, and it's not up to you. It's either there or it isn't.

There are subjects and activities which, if you pursued one of them, would awaken your sleeping vitality. But you may be ignoring them for "good reasons."

A woman I know liked to draw and was very good at it while she was still only in kindergarten. When she told her father she wanted to be an artist when she grew up, he said, "You don't want to be an artist. Artists don't make any money." He dismissed the idea with so much *certainty*, she dropped her interest on the spot. She cut it off, turned away from it.

Many of us have had a similar experience. We turned away from what really interested us and now we don't really know what interests us. We look around at our options and don't see anything interesting because the thing that interests us is behind us, so to speak — we've turned out backs on it and can't see it any more.

I know a man who liked to sail as a youngster, but let it fade out of his life when he became an adult. He thought about it once in a while but figured he would do some sailing "later" when he had a lot of money and extra time (dream on dude). He recently decided to take up sailing, even on a small scale, and he has come alive.

Boredom is death. *Interest* is life. Dig up that dormant interest. You know the one — you've dropped it or laid it aside for perfectly sound reasons. You might even feel it's childish to pursue it. That's the one! Pursue it, even a little, and your awakened interest will brighten your whole life.

If I was going to choose only one principle from this book that would do the most for your happiness, this is the one I would choose. Find something that strongly interests you, and get into it.

Pursue an interest that makes you come alive.

Follow your bliss and the universe will open doors where there were only walls.

— Joseph Campbell

If you always do what interests you, at least one person is pleased.

— Katharine Hepburn

Positive Thinking: The Next Generation

TRYING TO THINK POSITIVELY when you feel bad is difficult. Forty years ago, that was the best you could hope for. But since then, an enormous amount of research has been done on exactly how our thoughts affect the way we feel. This is the realm of cognitive science.

Researchers have discovered that when you feel bad, it is easier to be *negative* about your negative thoughts than it is to "think positive," and it is more likely to improve your mood.

The most important insight from cognitive research is this: When you feel angry, anxious, or depressed, those feelings are largely caused by irrational (unreasonable) negative assumptions.

Of course, circumstances call for some kind of response, but your response will depend on your habits of thinking. When you're in the habit of making faulty (irrational, unreasonable, unjustifiable) assumptions in response to certain kinds of events, you're likely to feel a lot of anger, anxiety or sadness in that area of your life.

Cognitive science says, "Rather than trying to think positively when you are experiencing negative emotions, find out what's wrong with your negative thinking."

If you've got strong negative feelings, your thinking is inevitably distorted, unsubstantiated and overgeneralized. Criticizing the assumptions behind your negative feelings *measurably* and *significantly* improves your mood.

When you find yourself making an unreasonable assumption and it makes you feel bad, *attack the assumption.* Check it for illogic. See if you're exaggerating or ignoring evidence.

Give your own negative thoughts the same treatment you would give the statements of a fast-talking salesperson: Question them without mercy. Don't assume that something is true simply because *you* thought it. Check your *own* thoughts against logic and evidence as skeptically as you would the thoughts of someone else. You are fallible like any other human being, and you are capable of thinking thoughts that are not only untrue, but also counterproductive.

If you've got the time, criticize your assumptions *on paper.* Write an assumption you're making — something you think is true about the situation, some assessment or opinion you have — and then write out all the reasons why that assumption may not, in fact, be true, and why it may be a supremely stupid thing to think. When I do this, I often use two pens of different color, one for the assumptions and one for my criticisms of those assumptions.

Once I have successfully argued with my negative thoughts and my mood improves, I find it much easier to look on the bright side, talk to myself reassuringly, expect the best, and all the other techniques classified as "positive thinking." Those techniques are best for *staying* in a good mood. Attacking negative thinking is best for getting *out* of a bad mood.

Think about this next time you feel mad, annoyed, frustrated, stressed, worried, or down-in-the-dumps. Pay attention to your thoughts and then *argue with those thoughts* on the basis of evidence and reason. The moment you recognize one of your negative thoughts as irrational, you will feel better.

You may have to argue with the same thoughts over and over again, sometimes for months, but eventually you will get in the habit of making more rational assumptions, and the more rational your thoughts, the less you will be troubled by the negative emotions your thoughts were causing.

When you are no longer burdened by unnecessary feelings of sadness, anger, and fear, you'll find your general mood and sense of well-being will rise to a new level.

Cut yourself free of needless negative emotions with the blade of rationality.

Criticize the assumptions behind your negative feelings.

If we all worked on the assumption
that what is accepted as true is really true,
there would be little hope of advance.

— Orville Wright

From Hope to Change

ACCORDING TO THE International Listening Association, within twenty-four hours, we forget half of any information we've heard. Forty-eight hours later, we've forgotten *seventy-five percent of it.* And we don't grasp everything we hear in the first place.

But these numbers change when what we hear is *repeated.* And the more it's repeated, the better the numbers look.

All this has a huge bearing on how you make changes in your life. You change your behavior by changing the way you think. But the way you think is as ingrained and habitual and as resistant to change as any physical habit.

So learning new ways of thinking and behaving — and learning them well enough to actually make a difference — requires *repetition.* If, for example, you find a book that really makes a difference to you, read it again and again. Make it an annual event. Every time you read it, you will come across things you'd forgotten about.

Audio recordings of information are ideal for repetition. Listen to CDs or MP3s in your car. Travel time and even traffic jams will be transformed from annoyances to extended opportunities to improve the quality of your life. Find an audio program that teaches you something you really want to learn well, and listen to the whole thing ten times. Actually mark off the number of listenings. You will be astonished at how well you know the material when you're done.

Telling your friends about something you've learned also helps cement the new information in your mind. The more you share it, the better you learn it. The effort and concentration it requires to explain something to someone makes it clearer in your own mind and more permanent.

There are always so many new books, new downloads, new shows, new ideas, new information — we know we'll never get to it all, but our curiosity constantly pulls us toward it. But keep this in mind: Most of that new stuff isn't very good. And even less applies to your situation. So when you come across something that *is* good and *does* apply to your situation, hold onto it with repetition.

When you come across a good chapter in this book that applies to you, read it again in a month. Write to someone and explain the idea to them and how you used it and how it worked. Post the principle on your refrigerator. Read it onto a digital recorder and listen to it in your car. Keep it in your life. Repetition makes a difference.

With repetition you can take a fleeting hope sparked by a good idea and turn it into an actual change in your life. Instead of that possibility fading with your memory, it can grow stronger and stronger until your life is changed for the better. The distance between hope and actuality is crossed by repetition.

To turn good ideas into real change, use repetition.

Riches

IN AN EXPERIMENT at the University of Georgia, students were asked to remember a pleasant outdoor experience they'd had recently. Afterwards, they filled out a questionnaire rating their feelings of tension, relaxation and alertness.

Later the students experienced meditation by listening to recorded instructions with their eyes closed. Again, afterwards they filled out the questionnaire.

Was there any difference in their feelings of tension, relaxation and alertness? Indeed there was. *Recalling a pleasant memory* improved their concentration and lessened their anxiety *better* than meditation! And meditation is famous for exactly those effects. The amount of research on meditation and its positive effects could fill a bookstore.

And yet something as simple as *remembering a pleasant experience* works even better. But there's more. Recalling pleasant memories also *strengthens* those memories. Every time you recall a memory, it makes the memory more real and easier to recall.

Every event you experience in your life makes a pathway in your brain — a pattern of connections between neurons. But the pathway is weak. If you never recall that event again, your memory of it becomes weaker as time goes on until it becomes almost impossible to remember what happened, even if the experience was significant.

Some people are unhappy *only* because they don't remember the good times. Researchers find depressed people have as many nice experiences as everyone else, but they don't remember them as well. They've gotten into the habit of reminiscing about the negative experiences, so those seem numerous and vivid, and they let all the positive experiences fade into the past. So it seems to them life is tragic and filled with misery.

There is an important lesson we can take from all of this. Make it a point to recall your good times. Think about them now and then. Reminisce with your spouse or a friend or one of your children. Reminisce by writing to friends and relatives. They want to hear about your good times anyway — especially recent good times — so let yourself go. Writing about them will strengthen your memories.

If you do this, when you look back on your life, it'll be easier to see the beauty of it, and your life in the present will feel richer.

Think back over the last couple of weeks and try to recall the small pleasures: the tiny victories, the little moments of kindness and love, the gentle feelings of satisfaction. Feel free to recall the big ones too, but you have a lot more small ones, and you'll probably be surprised to realize how many you have.

Make a habit of taking the time to remember good moments. It will make your life richer.

Money and wealth are great. Investments and property are wonderful. But when all is said and done, your memories will have far more impact on your happiness.

Reminisce about special times of your life: moments of love, of awakening, of turning points, of great insight. Remember the events that help give life meaning. Remember the times that have shaped your life, or that you want to shape your life.

You have had special moments when you saw how wonderful life could be or when you gained some unusual insight. If nothing more is done with those, the memory of them and the power of the insights can fade. Make it a habit to *deliberately recall* those moments. Remember what they meant. Remember what they *could* mean and your memory will help make it so.

Reminisce about the good times and the special times. Strengthen those memories. Store them up. They are your true riches.

Reminisce about the best times.

The pleasure of remembering had been taken from me, because there was no longer anyone to remember with. It felt like losing your co-rememberer meant losing the memory itself, as if the things we'd done were less real and important than they had been hours before.

— John Green

The Ocelot Blues

WHAT HAPPENS WHEN YOU let your mind wander? Studies have shown when a human mind has nothing specific to think about, it becomes chaotic, flitting from one thought to another in a random way. But if any mind — your mind, my mind — keeps wandering, before long, our thoughts will land on something that grabs our attention: some fear or frustration or unfinished business.

You know what this is like: Your mind sticks there, like a tire spinning in the mud, dwelling on the worrisome or upsetting thought, and it ruins your mood. This is what happens to a mind without a purpose.

Having a purpose on your mind keeps your thoughts from devolving into chaos and bad moods. You can't stop your mind from thinking, but when you have a goal to think about, your mental resources are less likely to drift randomly into upsetting thoughts. They have someplace to go.

That's why studies show that people are more often in a good mood *while working* than they are in their free time. It seems unbelievable at first, but it is easily explained by the need for purpose. Most people are more likely to have clear purposes at work than at home.

There's an old saying that "idle hands are the devil's workshop," but the important factor, the factor that gets you out of the devil's workshop, is something you need to do that compels your attention.

Remember that principle: Something you need to do that *compels* your attention. That's the key — think of it as vitamin P.

The human mind needs a purpose. It's like the ocelot scratching off his fur at the Seattle Zoo. The zookeepers didn't know what to do about it. They gave him a female, but he kept skinning himself. They changed his diet. They changed his cage. But he kept clawing at himself.

Finally, someone realized that in the wild, ocelots eat birds. So instead of giving the ocelot meat to eat, they threw an unplucked chicken into the cage. Sure enough, the ocelot — using the same clawing movements he was using on himself — plucked the feathers out of that chicken and stopped skinning himself.

Your mind is like that. It needs a bone to chew or it'll chew the furniture. It needs a purpose. And not just any purpose, but something that challenges you, engages you, something you intend to accomplish, something you want, something real and concrete. Your mind aligns around that goal instead of being pulled into negativity, and you're happier.

Find a purpose that enthralls you
and then actively pursue it.

The only true happiness comes from
squandering ourselves for a purpose.

— *William Cowper*

Argue With Yourself And Win

WHEN SOMEONE MAKES YOU ANGRY, it may seem that the cause of your anger is the other person's actions. But what really makes you angry is what you think the action *means*. If you look closely at the meaning of an event, your certainty about it will fade. You'll realize it doesn't necessarily mean what you think it means. This uncertainty will make your anger diminish.

Suppose, for example, someone interrupts you while you're talking and it makes you mad. You "know" the person is being disrespectful. On closer look, you see that: 1) an event happens, 2) you figure out what it means, and then, 3) you feel an emotion in response to the meaning you created.

Step number two happens very fast — so fast it seems the event directly caused your feelings. But that isn't so. And you can prove it to yourself.

Wait until the next time you get mad at someone. Then try to discover one thought you have about what they did. You may have to backtrack — do a slow-motion replay. Ask yourself, "Why am I mad?" Your answer is probably, "Because he did such-and-such." Ask yourself another question: "Why would *that* make me angry?" Your answer to this second question is probably a statement about the *meaning* of the action. Now you have something to work with.

Take your statement and look at it scientifically. In the above example, someone interrupted you. You thought,

"He doesn't respect me." Looking at that thought scientifically, you realize it's a theory to explain why he interrupted you. Once you look at it, you also realize *it isn't the only explanation possible!* Try to come up with other explanations: "Maybe he never thought much about interrupting, and no one ever said anything to him about it, so he's in the habit of interrupting people — those he respects and those he doesn't." Or "Maybe he interrupted me because he has a poor memory and didn't want to forget what he was thinking, so he blurted it out before he forgot."

You can never really be sure why another person does something. Sometimes the person *himself* doesn't know why he's doing it.

After you create two or three good theories (this will only take a few moments), your anger will fade, you'll feel better, and you'll probably deal with the situation more rationally. People will respond to you better.

Argue with yourself this way and everyone wins!

When you're angry,
argue with yourself *first*.

Anger is never without a reason,
but seldom with a good one.

— Benjamin Franklin

Constitutional Right

"ABOVE ALL," wrote the Danish philosopher, poet, theologian, and social critic, Søren Kierkegaard, "do not lose your desire to walk. Every day I walk myself into a state of well-being and walk away from every illness. I have walked myself into my best thoughts..."

Friedrich Nietzsche, the German philosopher, went so far as to say "All truly great thoughts are conceived while walking."

A walk taken regularly for the sake of one's well-being is called *a constitutional.* Kierkegaard and Nietzsche were in good company. Gandhi, Darwin, Emerson, and many creative (and long-lived) people throughout history took constitutionals often. You can too. Here's how to have a good one:

1. Walk at a pace that's easy and pleasant. Don't make your constitutionals do double duty as an exercise program. A constitutional is closer to meditation, but it's not a "discipline." It's more like a vacation, and that's exactly the attitude to have.

2. Bring a little pocket-sized notebook and a pen, but don't *try* to get ideas. Of course, you'll sometimes think of things you want to remember. Taking notes is a way to free your mind — once your idea is down on paper, you're free to forget about it for the moment.

3. Walk for longer than fifteen minutes. A half hour to an hour is good. Two hours is great. You need to do it long enough to let your mind relax. This is a temporary vacation from our compulsion to *do*, and it needs to be long enough to have an effect.

On a walk, you get a fresh perspective; you can find solutions to problems; you look at things more clearly. You become calmer, saner and healthier. It's easier to think because, 1) you have the time to think, 2) there's nothing else you need to attend to, and 3) your brain is getting more oxygen.

This way of taking a walk is aptly named: It's good for your *constitution* — your overall well-being, body and mind.

You have a right to some quiet time to yourself, so exercise your right. A haven of peace and sanity awaits you... only a few steps away.

Clear your head and relax by going for a long walk.

It is a peculiarity of humor in me, my strong propensity for strolling. I deliberately shut up my books...put on my old clothes and old hat, and slip with the greatest satisfaction into a little cow-path, where I am sure I can defy observation.

— *Ralph Waldo Emerson*

Why Ask Why?

A QUESTION THAT NATURALLY comes to mind when something goes wrong is "Why?" But it's a question fraught with danger. Research has repeatedly shown that the human brain has evolved to answer a question with whatever knowledge it has (no matter how little) and come up with a plausible answer (however wrong).

For example, ask why you're overweight and, without any problem at all, your mind can come up with answers. But all it can give you are theories. What's the "real" answer? Is it because you weren't loved as a child? Is it a genetic weakness in your family? Is it an evolutionary holdover precaution against famine? Is your mouth simply bored?

The problem with a WHY question is that you tend to get too many answers you can't do anything about. You can't change your childhood or a genetic weakness, for example.

There is only one good thing about asking WHY: It can be entertaining. It's intriguing. It's like a mystery and mysteries capture our attention like nothing else. But if what you want is to handle the situation well or solve the problem and get on with the business of living, ask HOW not WHY. It's more efficient.

Since your mind will try to answer any question you put to it, the *kind* of question you ask makes a big difference. So ask what you really want to know: "How could I get slimmer?" Or "How can I avoid this problem in the future?" Or "How can I solve this problem now?" Or "How can I make things a little better?" Let your mind go wild on one of those questions. The answers will be more productive.

With HOW, you go straight for a useful answer. You avoid getting sidetracked into what can become an endless search for "understanding." With HOW your answers lead to actions. And it is *actions* that solve problems and produce real change.

Instead of asking *why* you have a problem, ask *how* you can get what you want.

In all affairs, it's a healthy thing now and then to hang a question mark on the things you have long taken for granted.

— Bertrand Russell

Judge a man by his questions rather than his answers.

— Voltaire

Honest Abe

WE CELEBRATE ABRAHAM LINCOLN'S birthday (February 12), and we should. Lincoln was one of the few "great men" who really was great. Before he became president, Lincoln spent twenty years as an unsuccessful Illinois lawyer — at least he was unsuccessful in financial terms. But when you measure the good he did, he was very successful indeed. Legends are often untrue, but Lincoln was the real thing. George Washington never chopped down a cherry tree, but Abraham Lincoln was honest. During his years as a lawyer, there were hundreds of documented examples of his honesty and decency.

For example, Lincoln didn't like to charge people much who were as poor as he was. Once a man sent him twenty-five dollars, but Lincoln sent him back ten of it, saying he was being too generous.

He was known at times to convince his clients to settle their issue out of court, saving *them* a lot of money, and earning *himself* nothing.

An old woman in dire poverty, the widow of a Revolutionary soldier, was charged $200 for getting her $400 pension. Lincoln sued the pension agent and won the case for the old woman. He didn't charge her for his services and, in fact, paid her hotel bill and gave her money to buy a ticket home.

He and his associate once prevented a con man from gaining possession of a tract of land owned by a mentally ill girl. The case took fifteen minutes. Lincoln's associate came to divide up their fee, but Lincoln reprimanded him.

His associate argued that the girl's brother had agreed on the fee ahead of time, and he was completely satisfied.

"That may be," said Lincoln, "but I am not satisfied. That money comes out of the pocket of a poor, demented girl; and I would rather starve than swindle her in this manner. You return half the money at least, or I'll not take a cent of it as my share."

He was a fool, perhaps, by certain standards. He didn't have much, and it was his own fault. But he was a good human being by anyone's standards and I'm glad we celebrate his birthday.

Honesty makes you feel good about yourself and creates trust in others. It improves your relationship with yourself and with others. It's not much in fashion these days to talk about the benefits of honesty and decency, but the benefits are there and they are tangible, palpable, and worth the trouble.

Lincoln didn't talk much about religion, even with his best friends, and he didn't belong to any church. But he once confided to a friend that his religious code was the same as an old man he knew in Indiana who said, "When I do good, I feel good, and when I do bad, I feel bad, and that's my religion."

Honesty. It may be corny, but it's the finest force for good in the world, and it always will be.

Do some honest good in the world.

My country is the world, and my religion is to do good.

— Thomas Paine

The Uncertainty Principle

TWO SAILORS RAN INTO each other in a pub. Over a few beers, one of the men told the other about his last voyage: "After a month at sea," he said, "we discovered our masts had been eaten through by termites! Almost nothing left of them."

"That's terrible," said the second sailor.

"That's what I thought at first too," the first sailor said, "but it turned out to be good luck. As soon as we took the sails down to replace the masts, we were hit by a squall so *suddenly* and so *hard*, it would surely have blown us over if our sails were up at the time."

"How lucky!"

"That's exactly what I thought at the time too. But because our sails were down, we couldn't steer the ship, and because of the wind, we were blown onto a reef. The hole in the hull was too big to fix. We were stranded."

"That is bad luck indeed."

"That's what I thought, too, when it first happened. But we all made it to the beach alive and had plenty to eat. But now here's the real *kicker*. While we were on the island whining about our terrible fate, we discovered a hidden treasure!"

As this story illustrates, you don't know if an event is "good" or "bad" except maybe in retrospect, and even then you don't really know for sure because *life keeps going*. The story's not over yet. Just because something hasn't turned out to be an advantage *yet* doesn't mean it is not ever going to.

Therefore, you can simply assume whatever happens to you is "good."

I know that sounds awfully Pollyanna and maybe even dangerously goofy, but it's very practical. If you think an event is *good*, it's easy to maintain a positive attitude. And your attitude affects your health, it affects the way people treat you and how you treat others, and it affects your energy level. And those can help pave the way for things to turn out well. *A good attitude* is a good thing. And a bad attitude does you no good at all.

So get in the habit of saying "That's good!" Since you don't know for sure whether something will eventually work to your advantage or not, you might as well *assume it will.* It is counterproductive to assume otherwise. Think about it.

If someone ahead of you in line at a store is slowing everything down, say to yourself, "That's good!" They may have saved you from getting into an accident when you get back in your car. Or maybe because you slowed down, you might meet a friend you would have missed. You never know.

The truth is, life is uncertain. And even *that* can work to your advantage.

When something "bad" happens,
say to yourself, "That's good!"

Be All You Can Be

YOU USE ONLY TEN PERCENT of your brain. Have you ever heard that? It's nonsense. You and I use our whole brains. Ask any neurologist. There are no idle parts of the brain, no brain cells sitting around unused. For example, there are neurons in your brain stem whose job is to immobilize your body while you're dreaming so you do not physically act out your dreams and get up and run into a wall. Every part has its function.

Idiot-savants can be a genius at one thing, like mathematical calculations or music, but they pay for it with a corresponding *deficit* in other useful attributes, like getting along with others. What happens is that one function, like mathematical ability, takes over a larger percentage of brain tissue — commandeers it, so to speak, usually as a result of a brain injury at birth — but whatever other ability that part of the brain is normally used for goes wanting. What you often get are geniuses who can't have a decent relationship or tie their shoes or control their emotions.

Each of those abilities require brain space, and there's just barely enough with none to spare. Nature did not equip us with a bunch of extra brain cells. As it is, the brain is as big as it can get and still (barely) make it through the birth canal. If it were any bigger, natural birth would be impossible.

You could learn more, do more, be more, for sure. But there is always a trade-off. You could use every spare moment, for example, listening to language programs, and thereby learn ten more languages in your lifetime. But it would have consequences. You'd have less time to socialize, for one. And that would have other, possibly negative, consequences.

You could work all the time, always improving yourself every moment of the day, but no play makes Johnny a dull boy. It's a trade-off. Balance is the key.

So don't feel bad that you're not "maximizing your full potential." Devote some time to your betterment, but also relax and enjoy the ride. You're alive on the planet, breathing the air and capable of communicating with other fellow travelers. Enjoy yourself and appreciate your life.

Improve yourself, but also relax and enjoy life.

When you dance, your purpose is not to get to a certain place on the floor. It's to enjoy each step along the way.

— *Wayne Dyer*

Science of Happiness

HAPPY PEOPLE have something in common. It's not money and it's not fame. According to researchers David G. Myers, professor of psychology at Hope College, and Ed Diener, professor of psychology at the University of Illinois, happy people are healthier and share the following four traits:

1. They like themselves.
2. They have a high degree of personal control.
3. They are optimistic.
4. They are extroverts.

THE GOOD NEWS is that none of these are fixed — each can be cultivated. If you are weak in any of these four traits, you can become happier by strengthening it.

1. Like yourself more by doing better. Improve your ethics — when you stop fudging on something, you stop feeling bad about fudging. Also, increase your ability — when you are more skilled at something, you admire yourself more, both for your new ability and for the perseverance it took to attain it. And treat people better — when we help others like themselves more, it comes around and helps us like ourselves more too.

2. Gain more control of your time by directly seeking it. This includes reading time-management books and applying what you learn. But

keep this in mind: No matter how good you are, if you keep increasing the number of pans in the fire, at some point you'll start to lose control. Decrease the number of pans until you have good control. With practice you may be able to increase that number. But maintain control in the meantime.

3. Be more optimistic by studying Martin Seligman's work and the ATTITUDE section of this book. In his book, *Learned Optimism*, Seligman outlines the three key areas where a change will make a difference and tells you exactly how to make those changes.

4. Become more extroverted by studying and practicing the principles in the classic *How to Win Friends and Influence People* by Dale Carnegie and the PEOPLE section of this book. It helps to begin with the supposition that introversion is simply a lack of ability to deal with people. Then, remedy that lack. Carnegie's book is still on the bookshelves after all these years because it's the best collection of information about how to deal with people that has ever been written.

NO MATTER HOW happy or unhappy you are now, you can make your life a happier one, and you can do it one small step at a time.

Strengthen your integrity, get better control of your time, become more optimistic, and practice good human relations.

Making the Most of What You Are

ONE MORNING A SIXTEEN-YEAR-OLD BOY was kidnapped from his house by a band of knife-wielding thugs and taken to another country, there to be sold as a slave. The year was 401 A.D.

He was forced to become a shepherd. In this new land, slaves were not allowed to wear clothes, so he was often dangerously cold and frequently on the verge of starvation. He spent months at a time without seeing another human being. That alone would be considered by many to be a severe psychological torture.

But this great difficulty was transformed into something wonderful because it gave him an opportunity not many get in a lifetime. Long lengths of solitude have been used by people all through history to think, to meditate, to learn to control the mind and to explore the depths of feeling and thought to a degree impossible in the hubbub of normal life.

He wasn't looking for such an "opportunity," but he got it anyway. He had never been a religious person, but to hold himself together and take his mind off the pain, he began to say prayers — so many that "...in one day," he wrote later, "I would say as many as a hundred prayers and after dark nearly as many again...I would wake and pray before daybreak — through snow, frost, and rain...."

This young man, at the onset of his manhood, got a "raw deal." But therein lies the lesson. Nobody gets a perfect life. The question is not, "What could I have done if I'd gotten a better life?" but rather "What can I do with the life I've got?"

How can you take your personality, your circumstances, your upbringing, the time and place you live in, and make something extraordinary out of it? What can you do with what you've got?

The young slave said prayers. He didn't have much else available to do, so he did what he could with all his might. And after six years of intensive solitude and concentrated praying, he heard a voice in his sleep say his prayers were answered: He was going home. He sat up and the voice said, "Look, your ship is ready."

He was a long way from the ocean, but he started walking. After two hundred miles, he came to the ocean and there was a ship preparing to leave for Britain, his homeland. Somehow he got aboard the ship and went home to reunite with his family.

But he had changed. The sixteen-year-old boy had become a holy man. He had visions. He heard the voices of the people from the island he had left — Ireland — calling him back. The voices were persistent, and he eventually left his family to become ordained as a priest and a bishop with the intention of returning to Ireland and transforming it into a land of peace.

At the time, the Irish were fierce, illiterate, Iron-Age people. For over eleven hundred years, the Roman Empire had been spreading its civilizing influence from Africa to Britain, but Rome never conquered Ireland.

The people of Ireland warred constantly. They made human sacrifices of prisoners of war and sacrificed newborns to the gods of the harvest. They hung the skulls of their enemies on their belts as ornaments.

Our slave-boy-turned-bishop decided to make these people literate and peaceful. Braving dangers and obstacles of tremendous magnitude, he actually succeeded! Slavery ceased entirely. Wars were much less frequent, and literacy was spreading.

How did he do it? He began by teaching people to read. Students eventually became teachers and went to other parts of the island to create new places of learning, and wherever they went, they brought the know-how to turn sheepskin into paper and paper into books.

Copying books became the major religious activity of that country. The Irish had a long-standing love of words, and it expressed itself fully when they became literate. Monks spent their lives copying books: the Bible, the lives of saints, and the works accumulated by the Roman culture — Latin, Greek, and Hebrew books, grammars, the works of Plato, Aristotle, Virgil, Homer, Greek philosophy, math, geometry, astronomy.

In fact, because so many books were being copied, they were saved, because as Ireland was being civilized, the Roman Empire was falling apart. Libraries disappeared in Europe. Books were no longer copied (except in the city of Rome itself), and children were no longer taught to read. The civilization that had been built up over eleven centuries disintegrated. This was the beginning of the Dark Ages.

Because our slave-boy-turned-bishop transformed his suffering into a mission, civilization itself — in the form of literature and the accumulated knowledge contained in that literature — was saved and not lost during that time of darkness. He was named a saint, the famous Saint Patrick. You can read the full and fascinating story in the excellent book, *How the Irish Saved Civilization*, by Thomas Cahill.

"Very interesting," you might say, "but what does that have to do with me?"

Well...you are also in some circumstances or other, and it's not all peaches and cream, is it? There's some stuff you don't like — maybe something about your circumstances, perhaps, or maybe some events that occurred in your childhood.

But here you are, with that past, with these circumstances, with the things you consider less than ideal. What are you going to do with them? If those circumstances have made you uniquely qualified for some contribution, what would it be?

You may not know the answer to these questions right now, but keep in mind that the circumstances you think only spell misery may contain the seeds of something profoundly *good*. Assume that's true, and the assumption will begin to gather evidence until your misery is transformed, as Saint Patrick's suffering was, from a raw deal to the perfect preparation for something magnificent.

Ask yourself and keep asking, "Given my upbringing and circumstances, what *good* am I especially qualified to do?"

An aim is the only fortune worth finding; and it is not to be found in foreign lands but in the heart itself.

— *Robert Louis Stevenson*

THE WORK SECTION

Zoning Out

AT ONE EXTREME, WORK can be overwhelmingly stressful. At the other end of the spectrum, work can be excruciatingly boring. Somewhere in the middle, work is challenging enough to compel your attention and yet not enough to completely outstrip your ability. When you hit that perfect middle zone, work becomes a pleasure.

When in this zone, people feel creative, active, concentrated, strong and happy — more so than when they're *not* in that zone. Mihaly Csikszentmihalyi at the University of Chicago discovered that people reach this zone more often on the job (54 percent of the time) than in leisure (18 percent of the time).

Work has gotten a bad reputation, probably from the beginning of the 20th century when working conditions were especially horrible. But those days are over and clearly we have the opportunity to experience a lot of satisfaction while working. The key is *matching our skill* to the challenge confronting us. When challenges and skills are *well matched*, we enter the zone. When they are *not* matched, it's unpleasant — too much challenge is stressful; not enough is boring.

If you are experiencing stress and tension at work, the solution is to *increase your skill* until it matches your challenge. For example, a typist buried in a backlog of unfinished work feels overwhelmed and tense. The feeling of tension tells him something: He has *too much challenge*. The solution is *more skill*, so he asks himself, "What skill could I improve to help me catch up on my backlog?" Maybe his answer is "Typing speed." He buys a typing-tutor program and practices after work. His typing speed increases (and his stress level decreases) until eventually his skill level matches the challenge of the job, and his work enters The Enjoyment Zone.

To cure *boredom* on the job, you go the other way: *Increase the challenge*. The way to increase the challenge is to set and pursue goals beyond what is required by the job. In other words, get the job done well *and* accomplish other goals at the same time.

Let's say our typist's program of self-improvement worked so well that it's now a year later and he no longer has any backlog. In fact, he's getting all his work done ahead of time! His job is no longer stressful. Now it's boring.

Boredom makes you feel tired and apathetic. You feel like you need rest, but what you really need is *more challenge*.

There are hundreds of ways our typist could increase his challenge. I'll give you two. First, he could try to make his typing as *perfect* as possible: using the correct finger for every letter, never looking at the keyboard, making no spelling errors, etc. And then, keeping these high standards, he could try to continuously increase his speed. Second, he could look around and see *what other challenges* (related to the job) he could tackle — re-organizing, making systems more efficient, raising the moods of his workmates, etc.

Now here's the catch. You knew there was a catch, didn't you? In the pursuit of The Enjoyment Zone, your skills keep increasing. So you need to keep increasing the challenge to keep up with it or you slip out of the zone and into boredom.

But keeping a good match between skills and challenges isn't as hard as it sounds, and the result is more enjoyment, so it's worth the trouble.

And since increasing skills are usually associated with increased opportunities for promotions and raises, there is another possible side effect you might enjoy: More money.

If you're bored, increase your challenge.
If you're stressed, increase your skill.

Work banishes those three great evils: boredom, vice and poverty.

— *Voltaire*

Time Management Made Simple

A LOT OF BOOKS have been written about how to manage your time by eliminating wasted motion and saving seconds where you can. But that's how you make a *factory* more efficient, not a human being.

People have one main source of inefficiency: We're prone to get sidetracked or distracted from the important things that need to be done and somewhat lost in the numerous unimportant things we also want to do. So the secret of becoming more efficient is first, know what's important and second, avoid getting off track. These can both be accomplished with a single technique.

Of all the words written about time management, the most valuable technique can be stated in one simple sentence: Make a list and put it in order.

There are always things to do. Since none of us can hold much in our minds while busy doing other things, we need to write things down or we forget — or have the uneasy feeling that we *might* be forgetting. So you need to make a list.

Write down only the *important* things you need to do. This should be a small list, no more than six items. Don't clutter up your list with trivial or obvious things. This isn't a schedule book, it's a To Do List, and its purpose is to keep you focused.

You've made your list. Now, put the tasks in the order of their importance. Putting the list in order makes your decisions smooth and effective. You'll know what to do first (the most important), and you'll always know what to do next. You also know you're making the best use of your time because at any given moment you're doing the most important thing you need to do.

There's no need to rush around or feel stressed to be efficient. Feeling tense or pressured makes you *less* efficient in the long run by causing unnecessary conflicts with people, mistakes, illness, and burnout. You are more in control of your life when you are calm.

Make a list and put it in order. This puts your mind in order and puts your day in order. It's a good investment of your time because you'll get more done that really matters.

Make a list and put it in order.

A man who dares to waste one hour of life
has not discovered the value of life.

— Charles Darwin

Dost thou love life? Then do not squander time,
for that is the stuff life is made of.

— Benjamin Franklin

Sustaining Motivation

A woman emailed me the following message:

"I read what you had to say on enthusiasm with, dare I say it, enthusiasm. My trouble seems to be that I cannot *sustain* that enthusiasm for any one thing for very long. I have bursts of passion, set my goals way too high, flounder and I'm back where I started in that grey limbo that so easily and so often turns to depression and resentment.

"I know you will say that in a way I have answered my own question (it's not as though I don't think about it often enough as I watch my life pass me by — I'm 42) in that I set goals too high, but lesser goals afford me little or no passion at all.

"I am (ungratefully) dragging through a lukewarm existence in search of that sustainable fire..."

This was my response to her:

Thanks for writing to me. I had a similar problem for many years. The assumption I made was if my enthusiasm dropped, there was something wrong with the *goal*. What I finally realized is that enthusiasm and desire need to be deliberately maintained. There are two ways to go about it.

The first is to sit down with paper and pen when you feel your enthusiasm wane, and argue with your own thoughts. Doubts and fears and pessimistic assumptions can, without even knowing what happened, completely kill your enthusiasm. If it turns out your doubts are legitimate, fine. Maybe your enthusiasm *should* die if that's the case.

But almost always — like 99 percent of the time — when you put your thoughts on paper and take an objective look, you'll find you made some faulty assumptions. And these assumptions have occurred in the background of your mind up until now.

Put it down on paper, find yourself a different colored pen, and then argue with each assumption. Come up with all the arguments against them you can think of. Read your little dialog every morning until you can feel the power of those assumptions has died out.

The other part of maintaining your enthusiasm is to keep your desire burning hot.

Here's what happens: You think of a goal. You can think of many good reasons why it would be great to accomplish that goal. You take action. You get busy working on the goal. You plan your time, you break it down into tasks, you're busy with the tasks, you run into some problems maybe, and maybe not. But the point is, you get kind of *lost in the task*, and in the details, and in your to-do lists and you do the one thing which you must never do: You forget why you wanted this in the first place. You're not thinking about that any more. That is a big mistake. All your attention is focused on what you *have to* do, not what you *want*.

Even though you have thought before about why you wanted to accomplish your goal, that's not good enough. You can keep your enthusiasm high by thinking often of *what* you want and *why* you want it.

Keep a list of the reasons why this goal is a great goal to accomplish. Keep adding more reasons as you think of them, and review them often. Read your list daily, and even keep it with you throughout your day.

As mundane as they seem, these two ways work very powerfully to keep your enthusiasm from fading. I heard

Zig Ziglar say something once that has stuck with me: The reason motivation fades is that the world is full of de-motivators — the naysaying of friends, the problems that come up, the constant distractions, the temptations to go off track, etc.

But the worst demotivators of all are what we do in our own heads. Those two methods will help you make your thoughts work *for* you rather than *against* you.

Argue with your negative assumptions on paper.

Keep refreshing your mind about why you want your goal.

Ability is what you're capable of doing.
Motivation determines what you do.

— Lou Holtz

Of course motivation is not permanent. But then, neither is bathing; but it is something you should do on a regular basis.

— Zig Ziglar

Envision it Done

HERE'S A RULE we all know we ought to follow: Do the important things first. You and I know if we're doing something of secondary importance while we still have something of primary importance to do, we're essentially wasting our time — even if what we're doing is constructive, productive, positive, loving, or any other worthwhile description. If it isn't one of the few things that are important to us, then it's a waste of time.

Of course that's a rather extreme and absolute thing to say, and there are always mitigating circumstances and perfectly valid reasons why the rule shouldn't be followed all the time, but doing important things first is a rule few would argue with.

Important tasks are usually more difficult than unimportant tasks, so we tend to put them off. But listen: That's because we're thinking about what it will be like to *do* the task. And that's where we go wrong. Don't think about that. Think about what it will be like to have the task *done*. There's a big difference — a difference that can make a difference. It takes your attention off the part you don't like and puts your focus on something you really want: the result. That subtle difference will make the task more appealing, so you'll be less likely to put it off.

Instead of looking at all your books and notes stacked up there, ready for you to do some serious studying, and thinking about all the time and frustration and neck-hurting hassle it is going to take to do, imagine the feeling you will get when you finish, or when you sit down to take a test feeling confident that you know the material well.

What a great feeling! Keep *that* image in mind when you look at the stack of notes and books. You will get to it sooner.

And when you get to something sooner, you suffer less because you spend less psychological effort avoiding the task. You get to spend more of your time on the other side — satisfied that the job is finished.

That's it. It's a simple change that makes things better. Vividly anticipate the *completion* of important tasks and you will get more of them done.

Vividly imagine the completion of important tasks.

This constant, unproductive preoccupation with all the things we have to do is the single largest consumer of time and energy.

— Kerry Gleeson

The secret of getting ahead is getting started. The secret of getting started is breaking your complex overwhelming tasks into small manageable tasks, and then starting with the first one.

— Mark Twain

Use What You Get

I WAS AT A PUBLICITY SEMINAR recently and the speaker said something very useful. She suggested that when get interviewed on television, you decide beforehand what message you want to communicate to the viewers, and then, no matter what the interviewer asks you, make sure you answer with your message.

Of course you have to acknowledge the question and make the transition to your answer smooth, but, she said, no matter what, you must stay on what *you* want to say and not get sidetracked by the interviewer.

She was an expert in her field and said this was good advice. Some interviewers are downright hostile. Even if they aren't, they often have a different purpose than you do for being there. So the question becomes: "Whose goal will be achieved? Yours or theirs?"

Of course, if your two intentions are not wholly antagonistic, it's possible *both* of you can be satisfied.

The same principle operates not only on TV interviews, but in regular life too. The first and most important principle is to know what you want. *Know what you want.* It doesn't mean you have to step all over everyone to get it. But your wishes are at least as valid as anyone else's, and from your perspective they are *more* valid than anyone else's. That's the way it ought to be.

So take whatever you get from the world — your circumstances, the people in your life and what they're trying to accomplish — and use it to accomplish your goals.

To do this you have to focus on what you intend to accomplish, and go after it like a hungry lion stalking her prey. No matter what happens, *keep trying* to accomplish your purpose.

It takes some concentration and a little practice. But you'll be able to achieve your goals with more certainty. And you won't be drained as much by things unrelated to your purpose.

Your goals are probably honorable and valuable. Do not let them get shunted aside by pushy people or less-than-ideal circumstances. Take *whatever* the world presents to you and use it to accomplish your purpose. No matter what.

Whatever happens, use it to accomplish your purpose.

When I attack a role, be it TV, film or stage, the first thing I say is, I don't want to know anything. If it's good I don't want to hear it; if it's bad I don't want to hear it. The only thing either thing can do is distract me. I like to stay focused.

— Cicely Tyson

Stay focused, go after your dreams and keep moving toward your goals.

— LL Cool J

Do You Want to Give Up?

WE HAVE GOALS — we have things we want to accomplish. And we really *do* want to accomplish them; we aren't trying to fool anyone. But sometimes we give up on our goals. Why?

All goals have obstacles to their achievement, things in the way. These are problems or difficulties we meet on the way to the goal that we must handle in order to achieve the goal.

What makes us give up is when it looks like we won't be able to overcome the obstacles. They seem too big or too numerous. When we feel *sure* we can't do it, we tend to give up.

What are the alternatives to giving up? Below are three. They are stated simply. Please do not discount them because of their brevity or simplicity. The fact that they are stated simply and briefly merely makes them easier to use and therefore *more* powerful, not less.

> **Get help.** There are people who want to help you. Enlist their aid. The more help you get, the sooner you'll succeed. Sit down and make a list of all the people who might be able to help you. Maybe you won't ask them all, but make the list because it will help you think in new and useful ways about how others can help you.
>
> **Tackle the obstacles one at a time.** When you try to tackle all the obstacles, or just *look* at all the obstacles at the same time, it can overwhelm you.

The feeling of being completely outgunned can take the wind out of your sails before you even get started. Pick one obstacle — an easy one — and tackle that first. Don't even *think* about the rest of them. It's likely that after you've tackled *one* obstacle, you'll be in a better, stronger position to handle the next one, and so on.

Get some training or knowledge that'll make you more able to handle the obstacles. Read, study, practice. As you gain ability, the obstacles shrink in comparison. The stronger and more *capable* you become, the less of a *barrier* the obstacles become.

NEXT TIME YOU are overwhelmed by obstacles, try one, two, or all three of these alternatives to giving up. You'll find they work. Using them, you'll discover new strength and zeal to keep your dream alive and accomplish your goal.

Rather than give up:
Get help, tackle the obstacles one at a time, and get some training.

Law of Return

ON MY PAGE-A-DAY CALENDAR, I recently read this bit of coaching: "Render more and better service than that for which you are paid and sooner or later you'll receive compound interest on compound interest from your investment."

Of course it's ridiculous to believe there is actually compound interest accumulating somewhere in the ether, but it is extremely useful to *think* of your effort in that way because that thought *can make itself true.*

When you think that way, you will work hard and enjoy it because you are assuming you'll be compensated for any work you do. Why not work hard? Any money you're not making right away for your extra effort is earning compound interest for you. Your extra effort is an investment that will be paid to you eventually. So your attitude is good and you are willing to work long and hard.

And because you do, you will be the first one to be promoted. You will be the one the customer seeks out. You will be the one who is indispensable. People will notice the extra service you provide and it'll work in your favor constantly.

Your original belief in this maxim becomes true by virtue of your belief in it.

And look at what happens to a person who *doesn't* think that way. Imagine a person who thinks, "I'm not going to put out any more work until they pay me more." Now if you were the boss, will this be the first person you consider for a promotion? If you were the customer, is that the person you want to do business with? No! Not if there is someone who is giving more and better service than you pay her for. *She* will get the business. *She* will get the promotion. She is more of a pleasure to work with. Her rewards may not be immediate, but they will come. It's the Law of Return.

It is only human nature to want to do business with someone who is trying hard and has a good attitude. It's human nature to promote someone like that. They're obviously an asset. Many *many* people just try to get by. So when you work to accumulate "compound interest," you stand out...and your ship comes in.

Assume extra effort is an investment that returns to you with compound interest.

Talent in cheaper than table salt. What separates the talented individual from the successful one is a lot of hard work.

— Stephen King

I know you've heard it a thousand times before. But it's true — hard work pays off. If you want to be good, you have to practice, practice, practice. If you don't love something, then don't do it.

— Ray Bradbury

Personality Counts

A PLEASANT PERSONALITY is important for salespeople and shopkeepers, but what about the rest of us? Isn't *competence* enough? Doesn't *technical skill* count more than anything?

A team of researchers at Purdue University wanted to find out. They studied the careers of a group of engineering graduates. After testing and follow-up, the researchers discovered that those who had the greatest mastery of the *technical* material made only slightly more money than the engineers with the least technical capability.

But those who tested high in *personality* factors earned about 15 percent more than those with the high technical ability and about 33 percent more than those who tested low in personality factors.

Engineering is a technical field. And even here, personality makes a big difference.

Of course, in truly perilous conditions, where *lives* depend on skill, personality doesn't matter much. Or does it?

For Charles Houston and Robert Bates, the leaders of an expedition, the *most* important quality they sought was personality.

The expedition in question was the fifth attempt to conquer K2, the second highest mountain in the world. They needed a team of eight experienced climbers. What did they look for? At the top of their list was "a good personality."

Houston and Bates had learned from previous expeditions that certain qualities of personality can prove essential to a group's survival. They knew from experience that if they were to succeed, each mountaineer on the team must "be able to keep his good nature and add to the humor of the party when bad weather, danger, or hardships strain the nerves." Even here, even in harsh survival conditions, the principle applies.

No matter what you do or where you are, your personality counts. When you try to get along better with others, when you exercise or eat better or get more sleep to improve your disposition, when you learn to handle stress or conflict or depression a little better — it makes a difference. On an engineering team or at the top of a mountain or at the water cooler down the hall, it makes a difference. Personality counts.

Increase your ability to get along with people and improve your disposition.

He who has so little knowledge of human nature as to seek happiness by changing anything but his own disposition will waste his life in fruitless efforts.

— Samuel Johnson

R-e-s-p-e-c-t

IT'S NICE TO BE LIKED, but it is even more satisfying to be respected. And although it takes some effort, you can attain it. Here are three ways your effort can increase the respect you get from people:

Increase your competence. People will respect your ability and skill, as long as you are noticeably good. This means trying to be a jack-of-all-trades doesn't work. *Concentrate* your efforts. Choose a useful ability and hone yourself into the Mozart of that ability. If the skill is used at your job, your increasing competence may bring you a new pay level too. Work on improving your ability whenever you can. Become a master.

Use good manners. Without using please and thank you and would you mind, without saying hi to people and learning their names and interests, you will not earn people's respect. Even if you're competent, you'll be *resented* rather than admired.

Speak up rather than smolder. Do it with good manners, but speak. It takes courage to speak up, and people know that and respect it. But when you speak up, make requests rather than simply complaining. Don't say what you don't like about what's already been done; say what you'd like to see in the future. And think it through beforehand so you say it well.

Don't worry much about whether or not people *like* you. Concentrate on competence and good manners and saying what you need to say, and you'll get more than liking. You'll get even more than respect from others. You'll earn the reward that might matter more than any other: You'll respect yourself.

Increase your competence, use good manners, and speak up rather than smolder.

To free us from the expectations of others, to give us back to ourselves — there lies the great, singular power of self-respect.

— Joan Didion

Manners are a sensitive awareness of the feelings of others. If you have that awareness, you have good manners, no matter what fork you use.

— Emily Post

A Powerful Way to Talk to Yourself

THERE ARE MANY DIFFERENT ways to talk to yourself. One way, for example, is to reassure yourself. Before a party you might feel nervous so you tell yourself, "It's going to be fine. It'll turn out okay."

Another way to talk to yourself is to give yourself advice or instruction. For example, "At the party, I will focus on trying to draw people out and get them to talk about themselves."

Another possible way to talk to yourself is to put yourself down. "I look like hell. I'm a loser."

Another way to talk to yourself is to ask yourself a question. On your way to the party, you could ask, "What can I do tonight to make it genuinely fun?"

Of all the possible ways to talk to yourself, asking yourself a question is the most powerful. Why? Because questions direct your mind and set trains of thought into motion. Questions *generate* thought. And because they are so powerful, it really makes a difference to pay attention to the questions you ask yourself and to ask yourself good questions.

Asking yourself a bad question before a party, for instance, can create excessive anxiety and a negative experience. For example, "What if I can't think of anything to say? What if I embarrass myself? What if I'm a loser for the rest of my life and I never get married and live alone, shunned by the world?"

The what-if questions are creating a chain of anxious thoughts and images that produce feelings of anxiety. With thoughts like these running through your mind, you arrive at the party feeling nervous and withdrawn. You can't think of anything pleasant to say (because your own anxious thoughts are occupying your mind) and you embarrass yourself with your own awkwardness.

Keep this up and your dire predictions of a lonely life could come true — not because of any personal flaws, but merely because you never paid attention to the questions you asked yourself, and you never tried to ask yourself high-quality questions.

What makes a question high-quality? What makes a question a *good* question? The result. A high-quality question has a good *result.* It focuses your attention on something that makes you effective. It directs your mind to something that helps you successfully handle the situation. A question is good if it leads to a good result.

> Bad question: What if they don't like me?
>
> Good question: How can I help the others here have a good time?
>
> Bad question: What if I fail to accomplish my goal?
>
> Good question: What's the most important thing I could do to make sure I accomplish my goal?

Ask yourself, "What *result* do I want?" And when you decide on a result, ask yourself, "What question can I ponder that would help me achieve that result?" Don't settle for the first thing that pops into your head! Think about it.

Make a list. Force yourself to come up with ten good possible questions. For something important, try twenty-five.

Then choose the best question — the one that will produce the best *result* — and practice asking yourself that question. *Literally* practice. Ask that question many times. Get used to asking it. Make it familiar and comfortable and automatic.

There are certain times when it would help to ask yourself that question. *Practice* asking that question *at those times*.

For example, when Katie is preparing for an interview, she doesn't want to obsess about her usual question, "What if I make a fool of myself in the interview?" She is fully aware that this question would not put her in the best frame of mind for an interview. The question would probably distract her and make her anxious, reducing her chance of getting the job.

She decides a good question to ponder is, "How can I help these people?" That will put her in a great attitude for an interview. That's a question that will produce a good result.

So while she is getting dressed for the interview, she asks herself the question. She ponders it. When her mind wanders, she comes back to the question again and again.

And in the car, on the way to the interview, she thinks about it some more, trying to think of ways she can help her future employers.

Whenever her mind drifts to her worries, she asks herself, "Yes, but how can I help these people?" And even walking into the interview, she is wondering how she can help them.

What do you think would be the difference between Katie sitting down for an interview wondering, "What if I make a fool of myself?" versus sitting down wondering, "How can I help these people?" What kind of difference would she have in *attitude?* In her *demeanor?* In her level of stress hormones? In her *focus* — outward versus inward focus?

I think you can see it would be a large and visibly obvious difference. The second question would make her more effective in the interview. The second question is more likely to lead to a good result.

Asking yourself a good question is a powerful tool. What great things do you think it can help *you* achieve? Good question.

Ask yourself questions that lead to good results.

Successful people ask better questions,
and as a result, they get better answers.

— Anthony Robbins

A major stimulant to creative thinking is focused questions. There is something about a well-worded question that often penetrates to the heart of the matter and triggers new ideas and insights.

— Brian Tracy

Does Positive Thinking Work?

THE MOST COMMON QUESTION people ask me is about positive thinking. People say things like, "I really try to think positive, but I am overwhelmed by negativity." Many people have concluded that either positive thinking doesn't work, or they are somehow not *trying* hard enough.

The fact is, positive thinking can be a very effective tool in the right circumstances, but it has to be done the right way and at the right time. But before I get into that, I want to get off on the right foot and say it is best to consider positive thinking as *self-coaching.*

Self-coaching is a more accurate description of what you're trying to do, and it's the name many researchers use when they try to determine if it makes any difference. And they've discovered it can indeed make a great deal of difference.

For example, in a study of Olympic gymnasts, those who made the U.S. men's gymnastics team employed more self-coaching than those who weren't able to qualify.

In a different study, "positive self-talk" made it easier for a gymnast to do well.

Researcher Susan Jackson did a study on twenty-eight elite athletes from seven different sports. She found that confidence, ability to focus, and level of motivation were key factors in their ability to consistently succeed. Self-coaching can enhance all three of those key factors.

Self-coaching can make a difference. But you must do it *well.* To make it work for you, apply the following principles:

1. Coach toward a purpose. The first step in self-coaching is to make sure you know what you're coaching *toward.* Clearly define your purpose, and make it simple. Don't complicate it and don't attempt several purposes at once. Yogi Berra said, "When you come to a fork in the road, take it." That's funny because you can't take a fork in the road. You can't go two directions at once. Before you can coach yourself, you must choose a direction.

Championship race-walker Curt Clausen starts preparing for competitions by saying, "I want to win this race." Does that seem too basic? Setting your goal clearly in your mind is an important, basic first step that should not be overlooked.

Clausen then makes a detailed plan — what he's going to do and when. He *talks to himself* about what he'll do if this or that happens. He makes a plan for how he will achieve his purpose. And he runs that plan through his head over and over during the race.

He is self-coaching toward a purpose — not just trying to *feel good* or *look positive.* He's trying to *accomplish* something and his self-coaching is toward that end. That is the first and most important key of "positive thinking." It's got to be toward a clear goal.

2. Give yourself commands. Literally *tell yourself* what to do. Step back from the situation and think about what you need to do, and tell yourself, for example, "Okay, relax. Take a deep breath. Good. Now just walk over there and introduce yourself. Keep your face relaxed, etc."

Kayak champions Kathy Ann Colin and her pair teammate, Tamara Jenkins, were having trouble balancing. Their warm-up before the qualifying competition for the 2000 Olympics was awful. Colin had an additional distraction because her parents had been robbed at the airport when they flew in.

Colin and Jenkins both felt scattered and nervous. But before the race, Colin turned to Jenkins and said, "We can do this. Focus and relax and don't worry about anything else." It worked.

Coach yourself with commands — but not necessarily in a commanding or domineering way. Do it like a hypnotist giving commands: Gentle and confident.

And use the right *tone of voice* (you have a tone of voice inside your head) because even if you are encouraging yourself or giving yourself advice, your own internal voice can rub you the wrong way and ruin the good effect.

Don't yell angrily at yourself unless that creates the effect you want. Simply changing your own tone when you talk to yourself can make your coaching more effective.

3. Give yourself advice. Look at your circumstance the way you might see it if a friend of yours was in a similar situation. And then advise yourself the way you would advise your friend. Be kind and gentle. Reassure yourself and use your good common sense. Give yourself your best advice and then follow it.

4. Give yourself encouragement. It makes a difference to tell yourself, "I can do this." That's all encouragement is — the basic message "you can do it." This is what people call "belief in yourself." It's nothing more than coaching yourself, encouraging yourself, saying to yourself, "I can do it."

Talk to yourself in a confident and reassuring way. Encourage yourself *without* overstating your case or *trying to feel enthusiastic*. Talk to yourself genuinely and sincerely, like you would talk to your best friend, and give yourself some encouragement.

5. Give yourself reasons. Remind yourself of the reasons why you can overcome this obstacle. Tell yourself about your past successes. Remind yourself of your strengths. Also, remind yourself why you really want it. Think up *new* reasons. Good reasons will motivate you and strengthen your determination.

6. Aim for your favorite positive emotion. Wanting to have a positive attitude when dealing with others — kids, neighbors, the clerk at the store — people often do it by acting cheerful and enthusiastic.

But most people don't like the forced, phony feeling of trying to be cheerful. Try this instead: Aim for love. Love is a very "positive attitude" and it changes the way you *feel* to aim for that, rather than just changing your external expression. And it takes attention away from you and puts it out there on the other person. You'll have a better effect on the world. Try it and see what I mean.

Your cheerfulness can sometimes annoy people. But feelings of *kindness* will not annoy people. The only difference is what you're *aiming* for. Are you aiming at being cheerful? Or are you aiming at letting the other person feel loved or cared for? It feels different, both to you and to the other person.

Remember, cheerfulness and enthusiasm are not the only positive emotions. My two favorite positive emotions are determination and love. In my opinion, these are much higher states than cheerfulness or enthusiasm, and you'll never slip into a phony show of positivity aiming at these.

Please remember this. I believe this is the most common mistake people make when they're trying to "be more positive." They aim for *cheerfulness*. What they end up with is the *show* of positivity and a negative *feeling* of phoniness.

Aim for love instead. Or gratitude or feeling relaxed or determined. These are easier to attain and worth more than cheerfulness.

7. Try anti-negativity first. Find mistakes in your pessimistic assumptions. When you are in a negative mood, this may be the easiest and most natural way to be more "positive."

Instead of trying to pretend you feel positive or somehow drum up a positive feeling, you attack your negative thoughts with as much venom as you like. It works. Sometimes positive thinking is too much of a step. Try first using anti-negativity to get yourself up to neutral before attempting anything positive.

8. Keep it simple. When you coach yourself, keep your sentences short, to the point, and directed to action or bearing.

9. Repeat what works. You may have noticed that good coaches develop "sayings." They have certain things they say often, kind of like their pet slogans. As you coach yourself, you will often coach yourself the same way on the same activity over and over. So develop short, pithy sayings that capture a useful meaning. And use those in your self-coaching.

Once you get very good at coaching yourself, you can do a whole coaching session with one sentence and be back to the activity with a good attitude.

Have you ever read the book or seen the movie, *Alive?* It's the true story of a plane crash. Not all the people survived. The ones who successfully endured the incredible seventy-one day ordeal in the Andes mountains developed a few slogans they repeated often, giving them the determination to keep trying. "The loser stays," meaning the weak would die. "A man never dies who fights." "We've beaten the cold." And the one they said most often, "To the west is Chile."

IF YOU HAVE EVER THOUGHT positive thinking was bunk, try using these ideas and then see what you think. I believe you'll find that when it's done with skill, self-coaching can be very effective. It can improve not only the way you feel, but how effective you are at accomplishing your goals and dealing with people.

When you want to "think positively,"
coach yourself effectively.

Here's how:

1. Coach toward a purpose.
2. Give yourself commands.
3. Give yourself advice.
4. Give yourself encouragement.
5. Give yourself reasons.
6. Aim for your favorite positive emotion.
7. Try anti-negativity first.
8. Keep it simple.
9. Repeat what works.

A Terrible Thing to Waste

DO YOU SOMETIMES FEEL TIRED? Listless? Lack energy? It might be *boredom*. Some tasks are just plain boring, and when your mind is bored, it starts shutting down or drifting off and going to sleep. To stay awake, you must engage your mind. Here are a couple of ideas to help you:

Move faster. This makes your mind pay closer attention in order to avoid mistakes. This demand for increased attention wakes you up, focuses your mind and makes the task more challenging. You can speed up without feeling unpleasantly stressed: Make it like a game. How much can you get done in the next half hour? Set a target and see if you can reach it. This makes a tedious task less boring and, as a bonus, frees up more time for things you *like* to do.

Listen to something. Everyone knows it's more fun to do physical work while listening to good music than it is working in silence. Music engages your mind to some degree. But there is something that engages your mind more completely: talking. There has been a virtual *explosion* in the publishing industry of books and seminars available as audio downloads. Many people who commute to work have converted that boring and otherwise unproductive time into *a mind-engaging education.*

The *amount* of material available is staggering. In the next few years, using only the time you spend driving and doing household chores, you could learn a foreign language, listen to countless great books read to you by the best readers in America, and transform boring routines into an opportunity to expand your mind.

What would you like to know more about? I'll bet someone has made an audio book on the subject. One company finds the best professors in the country and records their complete lectures and sells them as CDs or DVDs or downloads (check them out — thegreatcourses.com). What do you want to learn? What have you always been curious about? They might have a lecture series on it.

There's another kind of value to listening to audio recordings. Often it doesn't matter what you have *learned.* Even if you could recite it by heart, some practical knowledge matters only if you have it in mind. Ideas about human relations are like that. I have pretty much memorized the principles in Dale Carnegie's book *How to Win Friends and Influence People*, but when I am face-to-face with a real human being, I often forget them. The principles are not fresh in my mind — they are stored away somewhere. For *this* kind of knowledge, it's better to listen to a little every day. Then the ideas will be in the front of your mind when you need them.

USE THESE TWO ideas to make boring tasks more interesting to your mind. Move faster, listen to something, or both. A mind is truly a terrible thing to waste. Brains are made to be constantly interested. Brains aren't like muscles; muscles get tired when they are used too much.

Brains get tired *when they aren't used enough.* Brains not only get tired, but over time, they can become smaller and more feeble.

Research is now showing that it is a myth that people lose their mental ability with age. What they have found is that people who don't continue to use their mental abilities — people who don't continue to learn and grow — lose their mental ability with age. Learning and growing is for everyone, young and old alike. Even during a boring task, you can find a way to engage your mind.

During a dull task, move faster or listen to something.

Live as if you were to die tomorrow. Learn as if you were to live forever.

— Mahatma Gandhi

Self-education is, I firmly believe, the only kind of education there is.

— Isaac Asimov

"I Don't Know What to Do With My Life"

THERE IS SOMETHING you can do that would make you happy and make you a good living. You may not believe that, and in fact, it's not true. But it's not false either. It is only a useful idea to hold as you try to find your mission in life. Holding that idea will help it come true.

The perfect career for you: 1) needs to be something you like to do, and 2) it will have to be something worthwhile — something needed and wanted in the world.

If you don't like to do your work, you won't be happy, even when you're off work. Not only that, but you aren't likely to work hard enough at it to succeed. And if your work isn't worthwhile, it'll feel as though life is empty and has no meaning.

Here is a powerful method of discovering what your mission is: For the next two weeks, every time you notice you're feeling good about life and about yourself, take a moment to write out the answers to the following questions:

1. Where are you?
2. What are you doing?
3. Who are you with?

GET AS MANY of these written "snapshots" as you can in the next two or three weeks. Then go through them and see if you can find the commonalities. What are some general themes common to most or all of them? What actions make you happy?

Happiness is an indicator of where your interests and purposes lie.

It sometimes helps to have a trusted friend look them over too. She might see something you don't see.

Remember Ernest Shackleton, the expedition leader of the ship Endurance? When he was young, a shipmate of his wrote:

> "When he was on the subject that...appealed to his imagination, his voice changed to a deep vibrant tone, his features worked, his eyes shone, and his whole body seemed to have received an increase of vitality...Shackleton on these occasions...was not even the same man who perhaps ten minutes earlier was spouting lines from Keats or Browning..."

THIS IS AN excellent description of what someone can see from the outside. When you're talking about a subject related to your strongest interest, people can *see* it — you come alive!

Ask your friends to not only look at your notebook, but to tell you when they notice you brighten up significantly. It will give you a good indication of where your strongest interests lie.

Whatever you find as a theme common to the times you are happy and animated, you can assume it is in the direction of your mission in life. It is in a direction that is right for you.

Now *put more of it in your life.* Gradually add more of it...maybe an hour of it every week for the next month or two. Then make it two hours a week. Keep adding more, pursuing your interest. The whole tone of your life will rise, and you'll be happier.

Find something you like to do that is needed and wanted. Put more of it in your life.

Don't ask yourself what the world needs. Ask yourself what makes you come alive and then go do that. Because what the world needs is people who have come alive.

— Howard Thurman

Every job has some components which are unrewarding, unfulfilling, and often tedious. But there is no utopian job, no job made up only of the things we love to do.

— Leo-Arthur Kelmenson

Great passions are for the great of souls. Great events can only be seen by people who are on a level with them. We think we can have our visions for nothing. We cannot. Even the finest and most self-sacrificing visions have to paid for. Strangely enough, that is what makes them fine.

— Oscar Wilde

Sometimes You Shouldn't Listen

WHEN WINSTON CHURCHILL was a young man, his father concluded that Winston was "unfit for a career in law or politics" because he did so badly in school. It was a good thing he didn't believe his father. It is not unreasonable to say the outcome of World War II might have been different if Churchill had chosen a different line of work. Criticisms like this are not at all unusual for people who have succeeded.

Barbra Streisand's mother told her she wasn't pretty enough to be an actress and she could never become a singer because her voice wasn't good enough.

Conrad Hilton, who created a business empire with his Hilton Hotels, once overheard his father say to his mother: "Mary, I do not know what will become of Connie. I'm afraid he'll never amount to anything."

When Charles Darwin was getting ready to set sail on his five-year expedition on the Beagle, his father was extremely disappointed. He thought his son was drifting into a life of "sin and idleness."

George Washington's mother was a nagging, complaining, self-centered woman by all accounts. She belittled Washington's accomplishments and didn't show up at either of his presidential inaugurations. She was always whining that her children neglected her and she was especially enraged when her son George ran off to command the army for the American Revolution. She honestly believed it was his duty to stay home and take care of her.

In his youth, the late Leonard Bernstein, one of the most talented and successful composers in American history, was continually pressured by his father to give up his music and do something worthwhile, like help out in the family's beauty-supply business. His father was quite serious and persistent about this. After Leonard became famous, his father was asked about it, and he answered, "Well how was I supposed to know he was *the* Leonard Bernstein?!"

People may criticize you or make fun of your ideas or actively *try to stop you.* Often their efforts are only attempts to protect you from failure.

But failure is only a possibility *if you stop.* If you keep going, a "failure" is just another learning experience. And besides that, giving up on a heartfelt aspiration may be worse than failing. "Many people die," said Oliver Wendell Holmes, "with their music still in them." That's tragic.

So listen politely to the worries and criticisms of your friends and family, and do your best to put their minds at ease, but then *carry on.* Listen last to your own heart. You know yourself better than anyone on earth. Make sure your song is sung.

Listen to your own heart.
Don't let your music die with you.

When an objective is meaningful, joy is
a natural consequence of its pursuit.

— *Allen Wiesen*

Just Keep Planting

PAUL ROKICH IS MY HERO. When Paul was a boy growing up in Utah, he happened to live near an old copper smelter, and the sulfur dioxide that poured out of the refinery had made a desolate wasteland out of what used to be a beautiful forest.

When a young visitor one day looked at this wasteland and saw that there was nothing living there — no animals, no trees, no grass, no bushes, no birds...nothing but fourteen thousand acres of black and barren land that even smelled bad — well, this kid looked at the land and said, "This place is crummy." Paul knocked him down. He felt insulted. But he looked around and something happened inside him. He made a decision: Paul Rokich vowed that some day he would bring back the life to this land.

Many years later Paul was in the area, and he went to the smelter office. He asked if they had any plans to bring the trees back. The answer was "No." He asked if they would let *him* try to bring the trees back. Again, the answer was "No." They didn't want him on their land.

He realized he needed to be more knowledgeable before anyone would listen to him, so he went to college to study botany.

At the college he met a professor who was an expert in Utah's ecology. Unfortunately, this expert told Paul that the wasteland he wanted to bring back was beyond hope. He was told that his goal was foolish because even if he planted trees, and even if they grew, the wind would only blow the seeds forty feet per year, and that's all you'd get because there weren't any birds or squirrels to spread the seeds, and the seeds from *those* trees would need *another* thirty years before they started producing seeds of their own. Therefore, it would take approximately *twenty thousand years* to revegetate that six-square-mile piece of earth. His teachers told him it would be a waste of his life to try to do it. It just couldn't be done.

So he tried to go on with his life. He got a job operating heavy equipment, got married, and had some kids. But his dream would not die.

He kept studying up on the subject, and he kept thinking about it. And then one night he got up and took some action. He did what he could with what he had.

This was an important turning point. As Samuel Johnson wrote, "It is common to overlook what is near by keeping the eye fixed on something remote. In the same manner, present opportunities are neglected and attainable good is slighted by minds busied in extensive ranges."

Paul stopped busying his mind in extensive ranges and looked at what opportunities for *attainable good* were right in front of him.

Under the cover of darkness, he sneaked out into the wasteland with a backpack full of seedlings and started planting. For seven hours he planted seedlings.

He did it again a week later.

And every week, he made his secret journey into the wasteland and planted trees and shrubs and grass.

But most of it died.

For *fifteen years* he did this. When a whole valley of his fir seedlings burned to the ground because of a careless sheep-herder, Paul broke down and wept. Then he got up and kept planting.

Freezing winds and blistering heat, landslides and floods and fires destroyed his work time and time again. But he kept planting.

One night he found a highway crew had come and taken tons of dirt for a road grade, and all the plants he had painstakingly planted in that area were gone.

But he just kept planting.

Week after week, year after year he kept at it, against the opinion of the authorities, against the trespassing laws, against the devastation of road crews, against the wind and rain and heat...even against plain common sense. He just kept planting.

Slowly, very slowly, things began to take root.

Then gophers appeared.

Then rabbits.

Then porcupines.

The old copper smelter eventually gave him permission, and later, as times were changing and there was political pressure to clean up the environment, the company actually *hired* Paul to do what he was already doing, and they provided him with machinery and crews to work with. Progress accelerated.

Now the place is fourteen thousand acres of trees and grass and bushes, rich with elk and eagles, and Paul Rokich has received almost every environmental award Utah has.

He says, "I thought that if I got this started, when I was dead and gone people would come and see it. I never thought I'd live to see it myself!"

It took him until his hair turned white, but he kept that impossible vow he made to himself as a child.

What was it *you* wanted to do that you thought was impossible? Paul's story sure gives a perspective on things, doesn't it?

The way you get something accomplished in this world is to just keep planting. Just keep working. Just keep plugging away at it one day at a time for a long time, no matter who criticizes you, no matter how long it takes, no matter how many times you fall.

Get back up again. And just keep planting.

Persist.

Somebody said it couldn't be done.
But he with a chuckle replied,
That maybe it couldn't, but he would be one
Who wouldn't say so 'till he'd tried.

There are thousands to tell you it cannot be done.
There are thousands to prophesy failure.
There are thousands to point out to you, one by one,
The dangers that wait to assail you

But just buckle in, with a bit of a grin;
Just take off your coat and go to it.
Just start in to sing as you tackle the thing
That cannot be done — and you'll do it!

— Edgar A. Guest

Be More Energetic

ENERGY IS A BEAUTIFUL THING. A person with a lot of energy can accomplish twice what someone without much energy can, and have more fun doing it. You get more life with more energy. And here's a way to crank up your engine: *Act more energetic.* That sounds like shallow, positive-thinking hype, but it's actually based on solid evidence. And it works.

When you act more energetic, it stimulates your body. Lying down is relaxing. Moving around is more stimulating. Moving around quickly is even *more* stimulating. It gets the heart pumping. It puts the mind in gear.

Our biology has evolved to fit a different kind of world than the one in which we now find ourselves. There were plenty of times in our prehistory when food was scarce. People who wantonly used up energy would be the first to die, leaving no offspring. The bodies following the prime directive *conserve energy* passed their genes to us.

But times have changed. It's no longer difficult to find food. If anything, food is difficult to *avoid.* Calories are everywhere, abundantly available. As a matter of fact, now a major concern for people in much of the world is being overweight.

Times have changed dramatically. There's no longer any need to conserve energy, but your genes don't know it. They've still got their orders, like a soldier in a jungle who was never told the war is over.

You can be more energetic, but you'll have to override your *feelings*. And you can do this. You'll have to essentially ignore the natural laziness we all share.

The way to override your body's prime directive is to *act energetic* whether you feel like it or not.

The truth is, you *are* energetic when you act that way, regardless of how you feel. Listen to what I'm saying here. You want to be more energetic? By simply *acting* more energetic, you immediately become more energetic *in reality*, in the same way that when you act ethical, you *are* ethical, regardless of whether or not you were tempted to do the wrong thing.

You can become more energetic in *ten seconds*. Simply start acting more energetic.

You don't have to *feel* energetic to *be* energetic. A nice bonus, however, is that often when you act energetic, it will rev you up and make you feel energetic too.

Experiments show that when people walk quickly, it speeds up their metabolism, making them feel more energetic, and this energetic feeling lasts for several hours after the walk. Acting energetic physically changes your body into a more energetic body.

So don't wait until you feel energetic before you act. Act first. The feelings will follow.

Act more energetic.

Burn Your Own BTUs

MIHALY CSIKSZENTMIHALYI has been doing some fascinating research into creativity and enjoyment for over forty years. And he invented a new way to study enjoyment. It's called the Experience Sampling Method.

Subjects in an experiment are given a pager and a booklet, and then they go about their normal lives. At random intervals eight times each day, the pager goes off. The subjects immediately stop what they're doing and fill out the questionnaire in the booklet.

Each questionnaire is identical. It asks what they're doing, where they are, and who they're with. Then it asks them to mark where they are on several scales of experience, such as one to seven to indicate where they are from "happy" to "very sad."

After collecting over a hundred thousand of these samples, Csikszentmihalyi had a huge fund of raw information. He began to wonder, "Are people happier when they use more material resources in their leisure activities? Or are they happier when they invest more of themselves?" In other words his question was, "If I spend my day off going to a movie and out to dinner (or using resources and electricity in some way), will I have a more enjoyable day off than I would if I spent the day gardening or reading or talking or doing something requiring just my own effort?"

Which is ultimately more enjoyable? Using energy outside yourself, or using your own energy?

What would you guess? To answer the question, Csikszentmihalyi and his colleagues went back through the data and sorted each experience sample by the amount of energy being used. They measured the material resources in units of energy called BTUs (British Thermal Units, the energy it takes to raise one pound of water one degree Fahrenheit) and sifted the data in search of an answer.

What they found surprised everyone. The *fewer* BTUs a person used in his leisure, the *more* he enjoyed it. Those time-off activities like watching TV, playing video games, driving, boating, surfing the internet, or anything that used electricity or expensive equipment were *less* enjoyable than self-powered activities like conversing with a friend, working on a hobby, training a dog, or gardening.

This goes against our intuitions, or what we naturally assume is most enjoyable. It seems so obvious you don't even need to say it that you would have more fun cruising on a yacht drinking margaritas than you would building a bookshelf in your basement.

"Everybody knows" it would be more fun to go to the movies than it would to sit home and read a book.

But according to the research, that is not the case. Certainly those high-BTU activities are *easier* and more immediately appealing. But not more enjoyable. Or more satisfying.

When the pager went off and the participants stopped and checked how much they were enjoying what they were doing, they discovered something truly illuminating: The most fun things don't cost much.

Is this true for you? Test it. On your next two days off, do something that uses up material resources the first day, and the next day, have a friend over and converse or do something powered by your own energy. You'll see a difference. The activity might not be as titillating at the moment, but when your day is done, you'll be more satisfied with the self-powered day. You enjoyed it more.

Do you want some first-class leisure? Find an interest and pursue it. Turn off the TV and computer and iPhone and use your *own* energy. You may be surprised to find it doesn't wear you out but fully refreshes you.

This is extremely good news. It's good for your bank account, it's good for the planet, and it's good for your own happiness. Use more of *your* BTUs on your time off and the world will be a better place.

Use your own energy during your leisure time.

A master in the art of living draws no sharp distinction between his work and his play; his labor and his leisure; his mind and his body; his education and his recreation. He hardly knows which is which. He simply pursues his vision of excellence through whatever he is doing, and leaves others to determine whether he is working or playing. To himself, he always appears to be doing both.

— L.P. Jacks

Leisure may prove to be a curse rather than a blessing, unless education teaches a flippant world that leisure is not a synonym for entertainment.

— William J. Bogan

How to Earn More Money

WHETHER YOU OWN your own company or work for someone else, you can earn more than you now earn. The first question to ask yourself is "Am I providing a product or service that is both wanted and needed?" When the answer is yes, you can earn more money by increasing either the quality or the quantity of your service.

The hardest part of increasing your service is *thinking up ways to do it.* Sure, if you work faster and put in more hours, you will increase your service.

And if you take more care and pay more attention to your work, you will certainly increase the quality.

Those are obvious. But there will come a time when these things cannot be increased any more: There are only twenty-four hours in a day, there are physical limits to how fast you can move, and you can give no more attention to your work once you are giving it all your attention.

But it is possible to think of other ways to increase your service. It will only take some thinking.

Sit down ten different times in the next month and each time think up three different ways you could increase your service. Allow your imagination to go wild. At the end of the month, pick the best one and do it.

Another thing you can do to increase your earnings is to read books and listen to audio recordings related to your line of work, your health, or your ability to deal with people. Learn more about these three topics and it will help you earn more.

The first subject to study is the specific area or industry you work in. Every field has a history. How did it start? Who were the principle originators? And that's just the beginning. Libraries, YouTube, and bookstores, are all brimming with material on every conceivable subject.

Study not only the background, but also information that might make you better at your job. Take night classes. Listen to audio recordings in your car. Educate yourself. As you learn, you become more of an expert. Generally speaking, the more of an expert you are in your field, the more useful you are. And usually the more useful you are, the more money you can make.

Learning ways to increase your level of *health* will help you in two ways: First, your level of energy is closely tied to your level of health, and you can do more work with a high energy level.

Second, when you have better health, you tend to have better relationships with people. Have you ever noticed how difficult it is to be nice to people when you feel like hell?

Our health affects our moods, and our moods affect our relationships with others. And people who get along well with others, according to the research, make more money than those who don't. Their relationships are better with their bosses and with their assistants. They get more cooperation and consideration. In the long run, this adds up to more money.

Which brings us to the third area to study: people. As far as I can tell, there is no final attainment in this area. I've been actively improving my ability to deal with people for about thirty-six years now (and I was pretty good when I started), and I'm nowhere near as good as I could be. In other words, I can profitably continue to improve my ability to deal with people for the rest of my life, and I'll bet the same is true for you.

Learn about your line of work, read up on how to maintain good health, and constantly practice the fine art of dealing with people. These are lifetime studies. And do the hard work of thinking up ways to increase the quantity and quality of the service you provide.

Do these things and you will earn more money.

To earn more money:
Increase your service. Continually learn about your work, good health, and people.

The most important single ingredient in the formula of success is knowing how to get along with people.

— Theodore Roosevelt

The principle was right there — you couldn't miss it. The more we did for our customers, the more they did for us.

— Debbi Fields

The man who will use his skill and constructive imagination to see how much he can give for a dollar, instead of how little he can give for a dollar, is bound to succeed.

— Henry Ford

Master Tool

THIS TOOL WILL HELP YOU clarify your thinking, get rid of upsets, solve problems, organize your activities, and make you more productive. It's a simple tool, and you already know about it. But just as Dorothy had the way back to Kansas all along without realizing it, merely *having* the tool doesn't do the trick. You must know you have the tool, know what you can do with it, and of course, for it to do you any good, you must actually *use* the tool.

The master tool is making lists. Listmaking can be applied to a great many areas of your life. I don't know if there is a natural limit to the usefulness of this tool, but I will give you a few examples of how I use it.

One of the things that tends to stress me out is the accumulation of too much to do. I collect things I want to do much faster than I can do them. So I need to manage my time well.

The best audio recording I've ever heard on time management is Earl Nightingale's *Lead The Field.* He tells the true story of an efficiency expert named Ivy Lee who visited the president of a steel company to convince him that Lee's firm could help him manage his company better.

The president said he wasn't managing his company as well as he already knew how, and what was needed wasn't more *knowing*, but more *doing.* Everyone at the company knew what they should be doing, he said, and if Lee could tell him how to get more of it done, he'd pay Lee anything within reason he asked.

Lee got out a blank sheet of paper, and asked the president to write down the six most important things he needed to do the next day. It took the president about three minutes to do this.

Then Lee asked him to number them in the order of their importance to the success of the company. It took the president another five minutes.

Then Lee said something like this: "Now tomorrow, pull that piece of paper out of your pocket and go to work on number one. Don't worry about the others until the first one is done. Then go to number two. And so on. Once you've convinced yourself of the value of this method, teach it to your people, and then send me a check for whatever you think it's worth."

A few weeks later, Ivy Lee received a check for twenty-five thousand dollars. And the president wrote that what Lee taught him was the most profitable lesson he'd ever learned. Within five years, the company became one of the leaders in its field, and its success was largely attributed to that simple method.

I've done exactly what Lee recommended also, and it always clarifies my mind and helps me get more done. I immediately feel less stress as soon as I've written the list.

It takes time to make a list and put it in order but the increased efficiency more than makes up that time. Don't take my word for it. Try it, and then send me a check for whatever you think it's worth (wink).

Here's another example of how I use the master tool: When I'm worried about something, I use listmaking to help me think. When I feel agitated, I ask, "What's bothering me?" And I'll make a list of all the things that are bothering me. The list is always *finite*. That realization, all by itself, is relaxing.

When the worries are in my head, it seems like I have a lot of them, but when they are written down, I can see there aren't that many. And once I've got my worries written down and I look at them, many of them seem pretty stupid.

But usually there is at least one important problem on that list, so I take out another piece of paper and ask this question: "What can I do about this problem?" I write the question at the top of a page, and number one through ten on the page and then force myself to fill in all ten spaces with something I can do that might help.

Often the most original ideas are the ones I come up with last, as if I need to get the obvious ones out of my head before I have room to think something original. I've solved many a problem with this kind of list-making-thinking.

The ways I've used the master tool seem almost endless. I've made a list of possible courses of action to deal with a difficult person at work. I've written a long letter of the ten most important reasons I love my wife and gave it to her. I've made a list of my top seven values (I made a list of twenty and then by the process of elimination, got it down to the seven most important).

"We make lists so we will not forget what is important," says George Roche, president of Hillsdale College, "...if we chronically forget items like milk and bread unless we make a grocery list...isn't it also likely that we will forget items like virtue and compassion unless we make a character list...?"

The principle has wide application. How about the ten most important things you want to teach your kids before they turn eighteen (and then putting it in the order of their importance and begin working on your top three)? How about a list of the top ten things you're grateful for? How about making a list of your favorite memories and sharing them with someone you love? How about making a list of the most important personal qualities you want to develop in yourself?

The principle is: Make a list. (Or make a list and put it in order.) There are many ways to use this principle to enhance your life.

Why don't you try it right now? Get a piece of paper, write on it, "How can I use this principle to improve my life?" Write numbers one through ten and force yourself to fill in all ten with an answer. Pick the best one and try it.

Make a list.

The discipline of writing something down is the first step toward making it happen.

— Lee Iacocca

When your values are clear to you, making decisions becomes easier.

— Roy E. Disney

The Trouble With Troublemakers

WHEN SOMEONE AT WORK talks badly about you behind your back, puts you down, interferes with your work, makes you mad, or otherwise makes trouble for you, the natural tendency is to focus on *them*. You want to get back at them. You want to talk badly about them behind *their* back, put *them* down, make trouble for *them* in some way.

But consider the possibility that returning like for like is a mistake. Sometimes that may be a good strategy, but look at the three practical steps below — all of them effective ways to deal with troublemakers — and notice: None involve talking about, thinking about, or even speaking with the troublemakers *themselves*, because these often don't work very well.

Below are three things that hard-won experience has shown will work a lot better:

> **1. Do your work extremely well.** Think of your level of excellence on the job as a kind of sliding scale, from doing as little as you can without getting fired at the bottom, all the way up to doing your very best every second you are at work. At any given moment, you are somewhere between those two extremes. Move yourself further up the scale and you will feel more confident of your position. Doing your work well counteracts the feelings of insecurity a troublemaker can cause.

2. Keep your integrity level high. Doing anything unethical will increase the insecurity you feel. Conversely, the more you act with honesty and fairness, the better you will feel about yourself and about your position at work.

3. Stay in good communication with everyone else. A common response to feeling that someone is out to get you is *to withdraw*. But that's a big mistake. The universe of human opinion abhors a vacuum, and if a troublemaker says something bad about you and the listener hears nothing from you, guess what? The slanderous information will tend to hold the floor from lack of any other viewpoint. Your bosses and co-workers may be mature, rational people, but human emotions still influence their decisions, opinions, and conclusions.

Stay in communication with people — not trying to prove anything, but just being yourself — and the reality of who you are will help negate any rumors about you.

DO THESE THREE and the threat from the troublemaker will be minimized. You can't really get rid of such an element for good. That's the trouble with troublemakers. They are bound to crop up now and then, as inevitably as a bad storm. If you try to argue with them or fight with them or use their tactics on them, you will lose. They've been at it longer than you.

Do your work to the best of your ability, conduct yourself honorably, and stay in good communication.

Your position will be solid and the storm will pass over you without so much as a shudder.

**Do your work exceptionally well,
keep your integrity level high,
and stay in good communication
with everyone else.**

Four percent of Americans are sociopaths, meaning that they have no conscience, and this statistic probably gets larger as one goes up the ladder of success. At the top echelons of success in big business, sociopaths are probably even more plentiful. Most sociopaths in business are not physically violent, and they don't look like Charles Manson. They look like we do.

— Martha Stout

It is useless for sheep to pass resolutions in favor of vegetarianism while wolves remain of a different opinion.

— William Ralph Inge

The Spirit of the Games

I'VE ALWAYS HAD A DISTASTE for competition. I never liked the feeling of trying to outdo another person. But competition is a fact of life, from the lowliest worm to the executive on Wall Street. Competition is like gravity. We may not like it, but there it is anyway, having its effect on our lives, regardless of what we may think about it. There's nothing nasty about it — gravity doesn't care whether you hurt yourself when you fall or not.

If you have two organisms competing for a limited resource, say, a lion and a hyena competing for the carcass of a gazelle, if the lion doesn't want to compete or feels competition is wrong, then the hyena will eat and the lion will go hungry. If this goes on, the lion will die of starvation and the hyena will have many offspring. Nature is not being cruel. Competition is the way of the world. It's the way life on this planet became so complex and beautiful and amazing. It's the way your incredible brain evolved. Ultimately, competition is good. It makes things better. It forces improvement.

I'm a writer. There are places that pay for writing. And there are other writers in the world who would prefer that the money paid for that skill and effort went into *their* bank accounts rather than mine. The money can't really go to every writer's bank account. There's a *selection* going on. Certain things will be selected for and certain things will be selected against. It is a *competition*, whether I want to acknowledge that fact or not. And, of course, the ones who compete the best will always out-compete the ones who don't compete as well (or at all).

Competition can be an ugly affair, typified by the presidential elections with all the mudslinging and back-stabbing. Although that's obviously competition, so is what goes on at the Olympics.

The presidential elections are ugly, but the Olympics are beautiful — whether you win or lose, you can still shake the hand of your competitor in friendship. You can compete with honor. You can compete for noble reasons. You can compete for the sake of others or for a cause you believe in. The Spirit of the Games raises competition to the elevated place it should hold.

Consider it in this light and you can learn to *appreciate* competition. It's important because you must either compete well, or those dreams you have will not happen. Whatever your job, this is true. If you've had, like me, a distaste for competition, start changing your attitude now. Learn to appreciate and even *like* competition, because the truth is, if you can compete well, you can fulfill your desires. If you can't or don't compete well, or if you don't "play the game" at all, someone else will get the raise or promotion or position, someone else's view will hold the floor, someone else's vision will be realized, and your dreams will become pipe dreams.

It's up to you. You can compete, play well, and know you've done your best, or not. It's your call.

Learn to like competition and compete with honor.

A Lasting State of Feeling Great

THE ENGLISH POET AND CLERGYMAN Charles Kingsley wrote, "We act as though comfort and luxury were the chief requirements of life, when all we need to make us happy is something to be enthusiastic about." He was right. When you have something to be enthusiastic about, you can be in a good mood almost all the time.

If your job or school doesn't make you enthusiastic, you're probably stressed or tired when you come home and just want to watch a little TV or surf the internet and relax. You want some entertainment. You want diversion. But entertaining diversions will never make you feel happy and fully alive.

You could make plans to do something this weekend, and you might be enthusiastic about it all week. But then Monday comes and back in the grind you go.

What you really need is something *ongoing* and meaningful to be enthusiastic about. What you need is a challenging and compelling *purpose.*

Up until a century ago, simple survival provided just such a purpose for most people, and that's still the case for many in the world. But for you, it's no longer a challenge to merely survive. More than likely, the only way you will ever be challenged by a compelling purpose is if you *create* one deliberately. And if this purpose is going to make you truly enthusiastic, it must be something that personally compels you — a subject or task you think is fascinating or vitally important.

Pursue your purpose with vigor and you will be in a good mood most of the time. Things that bother most people won't bother you as much. You'll still have your ups and downs, but they will occur in a higher range. You'll still have to deal with problems, but you will handle them better. And your improved attitude will make your relationships happier and more harmonious.

When you have something ongoing in your life that you are enthusiastic about, the quality of your life will be noticeably better.

Pursuing a purpose is not comfortable, restful or easy. But it can be great fun! It can make your life deeply enjoyable.

Watching TV (or surfing the internet or whatever is your diversion of choice) is enticing, sure. It calls to you. It beckons. It's easy and enjoyable. But it won't fulfill you or make you happy. A purpose will.

Find a purpose you're enthusiastic about and get to it.

When you are inspired by some great purpose, some extraordinary projects, all your thoughts break their bonds; your mind transcends limitations; your consciousness expands in every direction; and you find yourself in a great new and wonderful world. Dormant forces, faculties and talents become alive and you discover yourself to be a greater person by far than you ever dreamed yourself to be.

— *Patanjali*

Wasting Time the Old Fashioned Way

RESEARCHERS PUT SOME RATS in plain cages, each one alone. Then they put some rats in bigger cages with other rats and toys to play with. The ones in the "enriched environment" grew smarter (they learned mazes faster). And when the researchers cut open their brains, they found that the rats in the enriched environment had bigger and heavier brains because they had more dendrites (connections between brain cells).

Mental ability — for rats as well as people — doesn't depend on the number of brain cells, but on *the number of connections* between those brain cells. And the stimulation of play increases the number of connections.

To refine their understanding, researchers put some rats in an enriched environment and some other rats in a position so they could *watch* the rats in the enriched environment. What they found is revealing: The ones who watched didn't get any smarter and their brains grew no bigger.

Studies on human beings are finding the same thing: Something about playing games that involve interacting with others face-to-face *increases brain power.* But *watching* people play games doesn't do it.

We are social creatures, and we are healthier and happier when we get enough enjoyable social contact. Impersonal entertainments like watching television and surfing the internet do not encourage face-to-face interaction, and they usually lack anything close to the level of challenge you can get from playing a game face-to-face with people.

Television programmers and the people who design commercials and ads don't want you to turn away from your screen and talk to anyone. You might miss an ad. So they try to keep it as compelling as possible. The end result is people can "be together" for hours on end, playing videogames or watching television, without hardly talking to each other. This doesn't satisfy our need for sociability or challenge.

The same goes with surfing the internet. Web sites usually make their money with advertisements, and you have to be looking at the screen and not interacting with the other people in the room in order to see those ads.

Playing screenless games that involve interaction between people — board games, charades, card games, tennis, softball, bowling, billiards, Barbarossa, Balderdash, Monopoly, Password, Pictionary, Cranium, etc. — can increase the connections between brains cells and between people.

But we all know games are a waste of time. The problem is, we *do* waste our time. We watch TV and movies. We play videogames. We check Facebook. We waste hours. Apparently we have a *need* to waste time, or at least to spend time doing something other than working, even when our work is enjoyable.

Since entertainment that doesn't involve any challenging face-to-face personal interactions with people doesn't enrich our minds but playing games does, here's the bottom line: Screenless games are *a better waste of time* than TV or surfing the internet or videogames or movies.

Here are two tips for replacing some of your screen time with games:

1. Mix it up. Different games require different skills. Your partners will be good at some, lousy at others. Mix it up and you won't win or lose all the time and you'll get better in areas in which you are now weak.

2. Play games *you* think are fun. The games that are likely to do you the most good are the ones you think are the most fun. If chess isn't fun for you, regardless of its stature in some circles, don't start there. Be guided by one criterion: Fun.

You don't need to find games that stretch your mind. You don't need to make a game "do you some good." As long as you're having fun, it *is* doing you some good. The benefit is in the fun. If you're concentrating too hard on trying to do something good for yourself, it won't be as much fun, so it won't be as good for you.

So go ahead and waste some time. Relax and enjoy yourself. But replace some of the time you spend looking at a screen with time spent playing games with others, and you'll be better off.

Replace some of your screen time with screenless game playing.

Taking Credit

WHEN YOU DON'T TAKE CREDIT for things you do right or well, it can cause a mild but debilitating form of depression. You might not mope around, but you won't feel as enthusiastic toward life as you could.

When you don't acknowledge yourself for what you've accomplished, you get the feeling that you haven't really *done* anything, and since you know you spent the day *doing* stuff, your efforts seem pointless and futile.

The solution is to make it a practice to ask yourself this question: "What can I take credit for?"

Think of anything in your life that you're glad happened, and look to see how much of it you can take credit for. What part of it was because of what *you* did?

Until you are in the habit, force yourself to do this every day. Ask yourself the question several times a day, and try to start noticing this simple fact: Much of the good stuff that happens in your life is a result of *your* choices and *your* effort.

If you're not already in the habit of doing this, here's what will happen: Over time, your level of energy and feeling of power and effectiveness will experience a resurgence. Your estimation of your own self-worth will rise up to match your actual worth. You will become more enthusiastic toward life. You'll have the feeling that you have been spinning your wheels for a long time and suddenly the wheels are gripping the solid ground firmly and you are finally moving forward.

You probably already take the time to blame yourself for your mistakes when things go badly. So be fair to yourself and acknowledge yourself for your positive actions when they cause things to go well.

Take credit where credit is due. It may be impolite to brag to other people, but it is sane and healthy to acknowledge your own accomplishments to yourself.

Ask yourself, "What can I take credit for?"

People who believe they cause good things tend to like themselves better than people who believe good things come from other people or circumstances.

— Martin Seligman

Vanity and pride are different things, though the words are often used synonymously. A person may be proud without being vain. Pride relates more to our opinion of ourselves; vanity, to what we would have others think of us.

— Jane Austen

Make it Happen

IN THE REMOTE JUNGLES of Southeast Asia on the Malay Peninsula, two aboriginal tribes were studied in the 1930s and '40s. The two tribes — the Negritos and the Temiar — were very similar. They both paid a lot of attention to their dreams.

The Negritos' attitude was *passive.* They felt they were the victims of evil forces. If they had a bad dream about a tree, for example, from that point on they would be afraid of the tree and its evil spirit.

But the Temiar taught their children that aggression in dreams was a good thing. They taught their children that they should *not* turn away from dream monsters, but *attack* them. The children were made to believe that if they ran away, the monsters or evil spirits would plague them until they turned and fought.

The two tribes were similar in many ways, but this one difference made the Temiar *psychologically healthy*, according to Kilton Stewart and Pat Noone, a psychologist and an anthropologist who studied them, and it made the Negritos psychologically *un*healthy.

In any situation, you can have the attitude of reaching, of trying to accomplish what you want, or by default you will become a victim — the effect of circumstances and other people's goals.

If you aren't *actively* trying to cause an effect you want, you will be forced by the aggression of others to respond, to react, to be *the effect* of their initiations. It isn't the perfect design by my standards, but that is the way it works out, whether we like it or not.

So make it a practice to think about what you want, what you think would be good, and then try to make that happen.

You'll run into resistance sometimes. That's okay. No need to resist the resistance. It's just someone else trying to make something happen too (or trying to prevent themselves from being a victim). Don't get caught up in it. Keep in mind what *you* want and continue taking steps toward it.

In other words, become less passive and more aggressive in your attitude.

Aggression can be a *good* thing. If it's aggression without anger or judgment, it can create a lot of good in the world. In fact, it has already.

Think about what you want
and try to make it happen.

If you do not have persistence then no amount
of education, talent or genius can make up for it.

— Stephen Richards

Forbidden Fruits

HAVE YOU EVER HAD THE EXPERIENCE, during a power outage or on a vacation, of finally having the time to really enjoy a conversation or read a good book and found yourself thinking, "Why don't I do that more often?"

Why? Because the easy entertainments and products of our modern world are always enticing, and you can think of more things you want to do than you *can* do, and, of course, there are always chores that need to be done.

Some famous authors have written their books while in jail. I've often thought, "What a great opportunity they had." They lived in circumstances highly conducive to writing (because there wasn't much else to do). And here I am, stuck in civilization with all its temptations. Aw, poor me.

But there *is* a way to create some of the same kinds of experiences without power outages or jail time. Human beings have been successfully using a simple and very effective method for thousands of years. It is simply to *forbid* things.

Today, for example, I have forbidden TV for myself. And I've already written more today than I have in the last week. It works. And there's nothing forced about it. I do not feel I *have* to write. I *want* to. Once I take away the nonstop seduction of the television, the most interesting and fun thing available, when Klassy is not available, is writing.

Forbidding a distraction simply opens up the time I have available to do the things I really want.

Try it. Take the thing you do that wastes the most time or creates the lowest-quality experience and forbid it for a day. You don't have to make it permanent. Simply forbid it for tomorrow or for the rest of today. I think you'll like the result.

What is your biggest time waster? Facebook? Internet surfing? Videogames? Try forbidding it. By just taking a break, you get a little distance from it. The addictive feeling it gives you is weaker, and you get the joy and pleasure of doing different kinds of things than you usually do. Sometimes you will even feel a sense of *relief* that it is off limits.

This temporary freedom isn't hard to achieve, so this is doable. And when you do, you'll gain a perspective on the usual way you waste your time, and when you go back to it the next day, you may find yourself with greater control of it.

This is something you can do any time, and as often as you want, and it will almost always benefit you. The technique is ancient and powerful, and it never wears out. Give it a try tomorrow and you'll see what I mean.

Forbid something for the day.

Lost time is never found again, and what we call time enough always proves little enough. Let us then be up and doing, and doing to a purpose.

— *Benjamin Franklin*

Life is a Meditation

...AND MEDITATION IS A METAPHOR for life. Meditation consists of keeping your mind on one thing. Of course, what happens when you try to keep your mind on one thing is your mind drifts onto other things. So you notice your mind has drifted, you're *tempted* to keep thinking about it, but then you let it go and bring yourself back to your meditation.

Although life is a little more complicated, it is much the same: You notice you've gone off the track and you get back on.

You can't have it all, do it all or be it all. To live happily, you have to narrow your purposes down to a few: certain relationships, certain important values, and a general purpose for your life.

Then the world and your own mind/body will continually take you off onto side-trips and distractions.

Salespeople, in-laws, your own desire for diversions and pleasures and entertainments, advertisers, people who want something from you (like your attention), and many more sources of distraction are constantly vying for your attention.

So you get off purpose. And then you notice you've gone off on a purpose that has nothing to do with what's important to you, and you let it go and get back to your own purposes.

For example, I was doing some work in my living room one hot summer night and I wasn't wearing a shirt. Two teenage boys who were skateboarding by across the street looked in my window and one of them said, "Hey, put on a shirt!" I was being invaded in my own living room. I ignored it. He said it again. It was clearly wrong, and I wanted to go over there and wring their scrawny little necks, or at least call the police, or do *something* that would show those two punks they can't get away with that with me!

But all of that has nothing to do with my chosen purposes. No real harm was done. It was simply another opportunity to either get off track or let it go and get back to my work.

Make your entire life a meditation. Less of your time will be wasted on things that aren't important to you and more of your goals will be achieved.

Notice when you're drifting away from your own purposes, and get back on track.

For me, I'm focused on what I want to do.
I know what I need to do to be a champion,
so I'm working on it.

— Usain Bolt

Vocabulary Raises

AS ONE CLASS GRADUATED from a large university, a group of researchers gave them an English vocabulary test and then tracked those people for twenty years. Strange as it may seem, those who knew the definitions of the most words were in the highest income group twenty years later. The researchers also discovered that the people who, in the beginning, had the worst vocabulary scores were in the *lowest* income group twenty years later. There wasn't a single exception. Does that or doesn't that strike you as utterly astounding?

Could this really be true? And can we extrapolate the conclusion that if you started now and increased your vocabulary, your efforts could eventually put you in a higher income group than you would have been otherwise? Let's look further.

In another study, the executive and supervisory personnel of thirty-nine manufacturing plants were given extensive testing. All of them, from the lowest level of supervisor to the top of the executive elite rated higher than average on leadership qualities. Between all the leaders, there was a close similarity in leadership ability. But there were striking differences on the vocabulary test.

Basically, the higher the person's score on the vocabulary test, the higher their position in that company. The presidents and vice presidents of the companies had an average score of 236 (a perfect score was 272). The average score for superintendents was 140. Foremen averaged 114.

Why? What's going on here?

Look at it this way: When you were young, you didn't know the definitions of very many words, so you didn't understand much of what people around you were saying. As you learned more words, your understanding grew.

Knowing the definition of even one more word makes a difference because if there is only one word you don't know, you'll often miss more of what's being said than that one word. The word is part of a sentence that you will not completely understand. The sentence is part of a paragraph. One unknown word can create a small gap in your understanding of the entire subject.

The most obvious way to prevent that gap is to always look up a word you don't know. The bad news is that you can't really do that while listening to a lecture and most people don't like interrupting themselves when they are reading to stop and look up a word. I know I don't. So the word doesn't get looked up, and some of the ideas are only partially understood because of it.

The larger your vocabulary, the less that happens and the more you understand what you read and hear.

The good news is that after you know a word, you are more likely to understand any sentence with that word in it *for the rest of your life.* Any effort you make to increase the number of definitions you know can have a far-reaching and long-lasting effect. Here are three ways to improve your vocabulary:

1. When you read a word you aren't sure of, look it up. Then create two or three sentences with that word in it. Using the word in your own self-created sentence is the quickest way to cement that word in your memory. It takes a little more work, but it is surprisingly effective.

2. Get vocabulary audio programs for your car and listen to them while driving, speaking the words out loud (this makes it easier to remember how to pronounce them).

3. Buy or make vocabulary flash cards and keep some in your pocket to test yourself in spare moments — while waiting in line, for example. You can pick one every morning and carry the card with you to work, trying to use that word in several sentences that day.

Take these three steps and, in an adscititious manner, you may see your income go from a flat line to an upwardly pointing falciform in the vespertine years of your life. Sticks and stones may break your bones, but words may get you a promotion.

Look up words,
listen to vocabulary audio recordings,
and use vocabulary flash cards.

adscititious: *added, supplemental, additional*
falciform: *in the shape of a sickle, curved*
vespertine: *pertaining to the evening*

– Webster's New Universal Unabridged Dictionary

Play the Game

YOUR JOB IS NOT A GAME. But when you approach it like a game, you're more likely to be successful at it, and you'll probably enjoy it more. But approaching something like a game does not mean being casual or unconcerned about it. Look at people while they're playing a good game; they are quite *serious* about what they're doing.

Research at the University of Chicago shows that games produce a condition called *flow*, characterized by absorption in the activity (a lack of thoughts about anything else), a feeling of control, and enjoyment. And one of the most common characteristics of flow is that time seems to fly.

According to the principle researcher, Mihaly Csikszentmihalyi, one of the reasons games can produce a state of flow so consistently is that the outcome of the game is not important.

We may really get into a game and the outcome may seem very important at the time, but we know that nothing is really at stake. We won't lose the mortgage, nobody will die, the college tuition for our kids won't be jeopardized.

But at work, there *is* something at stake. That means when we're working, we may be distracted by considerations about where the work is getting us and whether it's getting us there fast enough. What this means is that work becomes a means to an end and that means the end of flow because a requirement of the experience of flow is an involvement in the activity itself — a lack of thoughts about anything else. When a person is looking at the clock or thinking about her position or promotion in the company, it's enough of a distraction to prevent flow. Even wondering if you're enjoying yourself is a distraction. *Absorption* is what produces flow.

Of course, when most people are working, they are working for money. So the work is done as a means to an end. Does that mean we can't experience flow at work? Luckily, no. Even when you do something as a means to an end, you can learn to become absorbed in the activity itself and forget about where it is getting you while you're doing it.

If you want to experience more flow on the job, then, you'll need to learn to become more engrossed in your work. Learn to "get into it." If your job is stressful or boring, however, becoming absorbed is difficult.

If what you've got is stress, that means the challenge of your job, either physically or psychologically, is greater than your skills. The answer is to find out what skill you need to improve and work on that. *Increase your skill.* That's the answer to stress.

At the other end of the spectrum is boredom. If your job is boring, you'll have to find a way to make the work more challenging, interesting, or creative. It may take you a lot of thinking to figure out how to do that, but keep at it and you'll find a way.

During his research, Csikszentmihalyi found a man working on an assembly line, doing the same thing over and over every day, who had found a way to experience flow in a potentially boring job. He approached the task like an Olympic athlete; carefully working out ways to trim the time it took him to complete each task. By timing himself and shaving off seconds, he had become the most competent man on the line, and he also enjoyed his work more than anyone on the line. He wasn't focusing on trying to get a raise or gaining the approval of his supervisor. He was engrossed in beating his personal best. He was engrossed in the task itself. He had increased the challenge enough to allow him to be engrossed.

Find a way to become "caught up" in your work, *engaged* in it, *immersed* in it when it's happening. Get so engrossed in your work that you forget about everything else, like where it's getting you. It'll get you a lot farther that way.

Get so engrossed in your work that you forget about everything else.

A weaver who has to direct and to interweave a great many little threads has no time to philosophize about it, but rather he is so absorbed in his work that he doesn't think but acts, and he feels how things must go more than he can explain it.

— *Vincent van Gogh*

Self-Help

WILLIAM MILLER, A RESEARCHER in the alcohol-treatment field, wanted to find out what kind of treatment would work best for controlling problem drinking. He divided his experimental subjects into two groups and tested the treatment group with a variety of methods, including Antabuse (a drug that makes you sick if you drink) and counseling.

That was the treatment group. But researchers always need a control group when they test the effectiveness of a therapy. They need a baseline of results to compare to the results of the experimental group. The control group was merely given a short self-help manual and told to read it and do their best.

Many of the treatments worked very well. But, Miller says, "To our amazement, people in the control group did just as well as the treatment group." They thought maybe they had flubbed the study somehow, so they repeated it and got the same results. Still skeptical, they repeated the experiment *again* and, once again, *they got the same results.*

People who simply took a short self-help book home were just as capable of moderating their drinking as those who received the expensive and more extensive treatment. Why?

Much of the most effective part of therapy is simply *convincing* clients to change and telling them *how*, which is, of course, something the therapist could put in a book. The changes you make in your life have to be made by you. Even good therapy is largely dependent on the *client's* self-help.

Practical written advice can be as effective as the most expensive help you can find because the two ways to improve your life are:

1) do something different
2) think something different

And written material can help you accomplish both of those. All you need is a little motivation, and a book can furnish you with that too.

Do you know what this could mean *to you?* This book you now have in your hands may look inert. It may seem commonplace and ordinary. But it can really help you change your life. Use these ideas. Improve the effectiveness of the actions you take, and improve the way you think. Use this book as a spur to your own motivation. You can make your life better — no kidding. Are you interested? Help yourself.

Make your life better by reading helpful books.

The poorest man in the world is the man limited to his own experience, the man who does not read.

— Daniel N. Fader

If you don't read about things that interest you, you won't have any interest in reading.

— Adam Khan

Speedy Reading One Chunk at a Time

THE ABILITY TO READ FAST is made up of lots of little skills. You can use as many or as few of those skills as you want. The more of those individual skills you use, the faster you'll be able to read. Add all the skills together, and sure, it's dramatic. But who needs dramatics? A small improvement is cool enough.

Of course, when you learn to read faster, you can read *more*. But there's another benefit that might not be so obvious: Reading will become more *interesting*. You find the same difference between hearing a lecturer who speaks too slowly versus one who speaks at a comfortable but lively pace. It's more interesting. And by reading faster, you're making the process more challenging in a controlled way. And a challenge that is under your control helps you get into a state of flow.

Below are three basic techniques for increasing your speed. Pick one and try it in the spirit of fun. When you have that one going pretty well, add another one. After awhile, you'll have increased your speed...and probably your comprehension too (studies show speed alone can increase your comprehension). Here are the techniques:

1. Don't let your eyes regress. Keep them *moving forward*. They will have a tendency to go back a few words occasionally. That repeated backward movement adds up. When you stop doing it, your speed will increase a little. Studies indicate that re-

reading words like that doesn't increase comprehension anyway.

2. Constantly practice "picking up speed" as you read. Reading is a *skill*, and like any other skill, the constant effort to do it better keeps you getting better and better at it as time goes on. Push yourself just a little, but constantly.

3. Take in more words at a time. If you normally see two words at a time when you read, your eyes look at two words, move to the next two and stop to look at those, then move to the next two, and so on. Begin taking in *three* words at a time so your eyes make fewer stops, which increases your speed. Raise your challenge only as your skill increases. Keep it fun. Don't push yourself so hard it becomes unpleasant.

WHEN YOU FIRST start practicing a technique, you'll be conscious of using it and that may very well distract you a little from comprehending what you're reading. But keep practicing and the technique will become automatic, no longer requiring your conscious attention, allowing you to put your full attention on the *content* of the writing. At that point, you will have gained an increase in reading skill to enjoy for the rest of your life.

Don't let your eyes regress, practice picking up speed, and take in more words at a time.

Thousand Watt Bulb

HERE'S AN ODD SUGGESTION: When you're working, try to burn calories. Be useful, helpful, and as productive as you can. Even if your job is sitting at a keyboard all day, try to do it energetically and with enthusiasm. It may seem stupid, but give it a try before you decide. Blast out your effort like a thousand-watt bulb and here's what you will get in return:

1. You'll be *more* energetic, not less. You'd think it would wear you out, but that's not the case, as you can find out for yourself by trying it. You may have a pleasant sense of relaxation at the end of the day, as you would from some good exercise, but it won't make you tired. *Holding back* makes you tired. *Going through the motions* makes you tired. *Just trying to get through the day* makes you tired.

2. You'll advance faster. Of course, when opportunities come around, the person putting their *all* into the work (you, for instance) is going to be chosen over the people who are getting by doing as little as possible.

3. Your job will be more secure. Throwing yourself into your work with enthusiasm will make you feel more secure in a sometimes insecure world. And you'll not only *feel* more secure, your feeling will be an accurate perception of the reality.

4. You'll feel better about yourself. It feels good to do well. And you can look your boss in the eye and know s/he's getting a good deal. You can see that there are very few people you work with (or none at all) who give their all. The comparison between you and the rest of the pack will make it very clear in your mind you can stand tall and proud when your supervisor is around.

5. You will improve your abilities faster. Whatever skills your job requires will be honed more quickly when you're giving it your all.

THE HUMAN BRAIN and body has a default setting: *Conserve energy.* You know this from personal experience. It's probably hardwired genetically and kicks in with the onset of adulthood. You and I have a natural tendency to try to be conservative with our energy output. That's there naturally, but you're not stuck with it. You can override that default setting with a simple decision: Put out as much effort as you can.

Put the decision into action and before long, you'll forget. You'll be back to your default setting. When you notice you've gone back to the *conserve energy* mode, decide again to try to burn calories. Remake your decision again and again.

Blasting out the energy won't wear you out or make you tired. But it will make you feel proud, secure, and confident.

When you're working, try to burn calories.

As Good As Gold

ONE FUNDAMENTAL FORCE allows you to make changes in your life and turn good ideas into reality. The greatest idea, the finest resolution, the best plan are all useless without it.

What is this fundamental force? It is the power of *keeping your word.* It's the attitude of honoring the promises you make as sacred — even (or maybe especially) the promises you make to yourself. The good news is you can increase your ability to keep your word. You can make this power more available to yourself.

First, understand the fundamental role it plays. Recognize its power.

Next, don't commit yourself lightly — treat each promise you make as something you will do *no matter what.* Be very selective about what you commit yourself to.

And finally, renew your commitment every time you break your word.

Each of us has what Abraham Maslow called "choice-points" every day. These are moments when we have to decide, "Am I going to do the thing I promised myself and move forward? Or am I going to do the easy thing and break my promise and move backward?"

And if you break your promise, you arrive at another choice-point: Will you renew your commitment to be a person who keeps your word? Or will you give up on yourself and adjust your self-image downward? The decisions you make during these choice-points determine the direction and quality of your life.

The most important starting point is to *make a promise* to yourself that, from this day forward, when you come to a choice-point, you will choose to keep your word.

The more often you make the choice to keep your word, the more your word is worth. Eventually, your word is as good as gold.

Keep your word.

Never esteem anything as of advantage to you
that will make you break your word
or lose your self-respect.

— Marcus Antoninus

No one, by swearing, makes themselves an ounce more honest; any more than a man makes himself wealthy by counting his gold. Oaths may make a liar a liar yet again, having lied about the oath as well. But it cannot alter the worth of an honest man's word.

— Jake Yaniak

Getting Paid to Meditate

IN MOST DISCIPLINES of meditation, the first thing a student learns is how to concentrate. The Master gives the students techniques. In some cases, students may be instructed to count their breaths. In other cases, they are given a word to repeat over and over. Sometimes they'll hold a visual image in the mind's eye or focus all their thoughts on a candle's flame.

There are hundreds of different techniques, but they all have one aim in mind: to teach students to hold their attention on one thing and prevent their attention from wandering away to other, more interesting things.

But this is America. The meditation practice of sitting still for long periods of time may have been perfectly appropriate for an unmarried, childless Brahman priest who was a member of a caste that was supported by the government, but you and I have to make our own living. We don't have such an enormous privilege of time and guaranteed income. We need to be up and doing. And there's a lot to be done.

The ability to *concentrate* is the core ability, the essential skill. Control your attention and you control your mind. But the discipline to control your attention doesn't have to be done sitting still. It can be done with anything — including your job.

Your job can become a "spiritual" discipline. The practice is simply to *keep your attention on your work*. And unless it's a challenging part of your job that compels your attention, your mind will tend to wander, just as it does in meditation. You'll get distracted. You may get sidetracked with a daydream or playing a computer game or talking on the phone. In some studies, researchers found that while people were at work, fully twenty-five percent of the time *they weren't actually working.*

The practice of meditation is to bring the mind back to the task every time it wanders. Over and over and over again. This is meditation.

Do that with your work, and you are meditating. Do it often and you will slowly but steadily increase your ability to concentrate.

You can make any job challenging with this technique. Let's call it the Productive Meditation Technique. Simply do your job with the intention of paying attention to what you're supposed to be doing. When you notice you have gotten off track, get back to the purpose. Get crystal clear on the purpose and function of your job and the part it plays in the overall scheme of things, and then give that purpose all of your attention. Your mind will wander. When you notice you've strayed from the purpose, bring yourself back. Again and again.

Then *take the practice home.* Sweep the floors or *listen to someone you love* as a meditation. Whenever your thoughts wander, bring them back. Practice mowing the lawn with your full attention. Cook dinner with your full attention. Talk to your child with your full attention.

This ability to keep your mind here in this moment is not a trivial skill. It may not get you reincarnated as a higher being, but it will make you more alive right here and now.

When you notice your mind has wandered, bring it back to the task at hand.

You Create Yourself

I WAS TRYING TO WORK yesterday, but I was tired. I had stayed up late and gotten up late and I felt "off." When I realized what was happening, I decided to get back on track. I started paying attention to my work. I looked people in the eye and spoke with purpose. I decided to be a person I respect — not some victim to my feelings or circumstances, but a creator of who I am.

I set a standard for myself and then lived up to it in behavior. And my feelings came around. I stopped feeling so tired. I started feeling more purposeful.

But even if my feelings *didn't* come around, and they sometimes don't, it wouldn't matter. I can look people in the eye even when I don't feel like it.

You can do this too. It's not like I have an unusual amount of self-discipline or willpower. You can set standards for yourself and then live up to those standards, even when you don't feel like it.

Let's not be the effect of our feelings. They change too much. Set physical standards for yourself: What you will *do*, not what you will feel. Act ethically. Speak with intention. Exercise even when you don't feel like it. You cannot choose how you will feel voluntarily, but you can always choose what you will do.

Then, regardless of your upbringing or past habits or how much you drank the night before or the argument you had with your spouse this morning, take the actions you want to take. Be who you choose to be. It's up to you. You are what you decide you are at any given moment — not how you feel, not how you were raised. Those are defaults, like the default privacy settings on your Facebook account, and you can change them any time you want.

On some days, your defaults may be perfectly good because the circumstances and your feelings line up to make you act exactly as you wish. But the rest of the time, you'll have to take over the controls.

Decide how you want to act and act that way.

I'm always thinking about creating. My future starts when I wake up every morning...Every day I find something creative to do with my life.

— Miles Davis

Life isn't about finding yourself. Life is about creating yourself.

— George Bernard Shaw

Every thought we think is creating our future.

— Louise L. Hay

An Island of Order in a Sea of Chaos

THE MANAGER OF A LARGE RESTAURANT hired my wife and business partner, Klassy Evans, as a consultant. The manager was having problems that caused her a great deal of stress and she didn't know what to do about it. For example, no matter how many times the manager talked to certain employees, they still continually showed up late for work and always had a good excuse.

Klassy suggested something simple: Every time a person shows up late, assign them a cleaning task to be completed before they go home that day.

It worked. Not only were fewer people showing up late, but some things the manager *wanted* clean were *getting* cleaned. The restaurant was under better control and the manager was less distressed.

My son used to leave his window open and his heater on when he left for school in the morning. No matter how many times I told him to turn off his heater, he never seemed to remember. Saving my money wasn't very important to him. It's the vexing kind of problem commonly experienced by most parents.

I decided to *make* it important to him and fined him one dollar from his allowance every time I found the heater on and the window open.

Would you believe it? His memory made an immediate, complete, and permanent improvement after losing only one dollar!

You control *yourself* for the same reason you try to help your child develop self-control, and for the same reason a manager tries to maintain order with her staff: A person or family or organization with self-control is more likely to succeed.

The way to gain control is to set standards and stick to them firmly. Establish standards and *make them known.* Then *keep* those standards come hell or high water. Whenever you find yourself in a situation where you need to have control, remember this well.

If you're a boss or a parent, think hard about the standards you set and make sure you set those standards carefully. Once you've announced the standard and the penalty for deviating from it, hold to your promise without flinching, and you will have gained a new level of control. You will have derived order from chaos. The method allows your child or your employee to learn self-control and by doing so, you increase the amount of successful action.

When he was first put in charge of a regiment, General Grant found chaos and disorder. The men were dressed slovenly, they showed up late and there was rank insubordination.

Before you can accomplish something, you first have to establish order, and that's what Grant did. When someone showed up late for roll-call, the whole regiment went without food for twenty-four hours. A man was tied to a post all day if he disobeyed orders. When a soldier cussed, he was gagged.

Rules were established, cleanliness was created, and order was the name of the game. They could get on with the task of training and fighting.

Then Grant took these same men and captured Fort Donelson and fifteen thousand prisoners in one afternoon! That victory turned the tide for the Union forces.

Discipline is difficult. Our yearning for freedom bucks against it. But without discipline, little can be accomplished.

It's a simple fact: Ultimately, it's more difficult and painful to do *without* discipline than it is to buckle down and establish control.

Set standards and stick to them through storm and thunder. You will derive gain from the pain. Success will be your sweet reward.

Set standards and stick to them.

If we do not discipline ourselves the world will do it for us.

— William Feather

We must all suffer one of two things: the pain of discipline or the pain of regret or disappointment.

— Jim Rohn

The Samurai Effect

YEARS AGO I READ the book, *Shogun*, by James Clavell, about the Japanese samurai (professional warriors). A samurai gave total allegiance to his liege lord and would die for him without question. The whole system was filled with honor and loyalty and was very beautiful in that respect.

While reading the book (which took a while because it is a long book), I started treating my boss like my liege lord. What a difference it made! My attitude toward my boss changed and my boss's attitude toward *me* changed dramatically. Our working relationship became smoother, more enjoyable, friendlier, and more efficient. I did everything my boss asked me to do, to the best of my ability and without complaint.

Of course, if my boss asked me to jump off a bridge, I wouldn't have, but usually bosses don't ask employees to do anything but their jobs.

I've often seen a *different* kind of attitude in the workplace, however, and I'm sure you've seen it too. It can be stated as, "I'm not going to kiss anyone's ass." This attitude is characterized by arguing with the boss when asked to do something or trying to get away with not doing it very well, or doing it reluctantly or begrudgingly. These people, even more than the rest of us, don't like being told what to do, and actively resist it, which forces the boss to bear down to maintain control, turning the working relationship into an unnecessarily antagonistic contest of wills.

I've worked with people who got along great with everyone *except* the boss. And I've worked in places where I had a great boss, but my co-workers had a supreme tyrant for a boss — *and it was the same person.* My "samurai" attitude had changed my boss for me.

In a way, your attitude toward a person *creates* that person. Interact with someone with a chip on your shoulder and the person will usually respond defensively. Approach someone with friendliness and cooperation and the person is likely to respond in kind. We play a big part in creating the way most people treat us.

Do you want to stand out? Treat your boss like a liege lord and do what she or he asks you to do — cheerfully, without question, and to the best of your ability — and you will stand out.

In your boss's mind, you will contrast sharply with the people who don't want to be told what to do. And it'll be more enjoyable for you to be at work.

Create a boss you enjoy working with. In actual behavior, the difference isn't much. You won't be any more tired or worn out by it. But you and your organization will be better off when you adopt a samurai attitude.

Treat your boss like a liege lord.

An ounce of loyalty is worth a pound of cleverness.

— Elbert Hubbard

Unnatural Acts

HAVE YOU EVER WONDERED why your co-workers complain so much? Or why you find fault with people so easily? Or why you watch the news even though it's depressing? Why?

Our species evolved during the Ice Age (the Pleistocene epoch). In the last one or two million years, there have been four glaciations — four times when the ice advanced southward for a hundred thousand years or so, and then receded, significantly changing the climate again and again.

These ice invasions caused the extinction of many species. But not humans. Our predecessors lived through the harsh and radically-changing weather, famines, floods, fires, plagues, and the threat of deadly carnivorous animals walking around hungry. Lots of people died. Natural selection had a field day.

Let's speculate for a moment. During *dangerous* times, what kind of human would evolve? Would a happy-go-lucky, everything-is-fine attitude help one survive? I don't think so. Under those conditions, wouldn't the best survivors be those who compulsively noticed what was wrong and were constantly on the lookout for possible danger?

In other words, conditions would have selected for a critical, negative worrywart. A relaxed, easygoing pie-in-the-sky Pollyanna probably wouldn't last one winter.

Those people who survived are our ancestors, so those traits are built into our brains and hormonal systems. Even yours.

It is completely natural to notice what's *wrong*, what *doesn't* work, and what you *don't* like. It's somewhat unnatural to see what's good, what's going well, and what you like and appreciate.

But it's also unnatural to be toilet-trained. It's unnatural to have good manners. It's unnatural to delay gratification.

What comes *naturally* (like being negative) is not necessarily best. It might have been absolutely essential for survival a hundred thousand years ago, but times have changed.

Luckily, we are capable of doing things we don't naturally do — if we know it's in our best interest and if we firmly and definitely make up our minds to do so. One of the greatest talents of our species is that we're capable of doing what we don't naturally do.

You can *learn* to notice what's going well. It takes a deliberate, conscious effort. It'll probably never come naturally (that is, without thinking about it). No matter how many years you make that conscious effort, whenever you look around, chances are the *first* thing you'll see is what's wrong. And that's perfectly okay. It's useful to be able to see what needs fixing. But it also helps to notice the good stuff. You can start right now.

Today, deliberately notice something you like about the company you work for and tell somebody. Then take a good look at your co-workers and find something you honestly appreciate about someone and tell that person you appreciate it. Then talk about someone behind her back — talk about what you admire and respect about her.

Make this effort a couple of times a day and your relationships will work better. You'll also be in a good mood more often.

Set a goal at the beginning of the day. How many sincere acknowledgments will you give today? Don't make your goal too big — you have work to do too. But create some way of keeping track. For example, you could put five pennies in your *left* pocket and every time you make a good acknowledgment, move one penny to your *right* pocket. Try to move all of them that day.

Make a regular practice of this and the atmosphere where you work will change. The people around you will feel more noticed and appreciated and liked. And they will treat *you* with more appreciation in return. All you need to do is commit some unnatural acts.

Notice something you appreciate and tell someone.

The aim of life is appreciation; there is no sense in not appreciating things; and there is no sense in having more of them if you have less appreciation of them.

— *Gilbert K. Chesterton*

I can live for two months on a good compliment.

— *Mark Twain*

The Shortest Distance

WHEN IT COMES TO SOLVING problems, using a formal procedure works better than letting your mind wander, so I have one for you. It involves four steps, and you do them in order. These steps are ancient. You could almost say this is *the* method to solve a problem. Anything else is less efficient and less effective. When you look them over you may think this is all very obvious and you can easily see why this method will work. But the important thing is *using it.* When you are confronting a problem, use this method:

1. Clarify the problem. Attempt to write down what the problem is, specifically. Writing it down is better than doing it in your head. Use a lot of paper on this one; it's an important process. Write something down, then try to improve on it. Keep working until you have a clear, simple statement of the problem.

2. List the causes. What has caused this problem? Usually a problem has more than one cause. List them all.

3. Create possible solutions. This is where you can use your imagination. During this stage, first come up with all the ideas you can think of. Then kick back and relax. Use your imagination. Let your mind ponder the problem in its own way, as if you were daydreaming about possible solutions. Look at it from different perspectives. How would an old sea captain look at this problem? How would Gandhi look at this problem? You don't know how those people would *actually* look at the problem, of course, but you can use your imagination and that will get you out of your habitual point of view. Let your mind wander, but keep bringing it back to the problem. Don't *work* at it. Do it in a way that's playful and fun. And stop every once in a while and jot down some ideas.

4. Select your favorite solution and try it. You now have a collection of possible solutions, and reading through them probably sparked some more ideas. Write them all down. Then look over your ideas and choose what you think is the finest solution among them. Now put it into action.

Your solution won't always work. No big deal if it doesn't — you have others to try. Take this step-by-step approach and you'll gain traction and equilibrium and *a feeling of control* — something that really helps when you've got a problem to deal with.

Problems are an important part of life, and it's always in your best interest to improve your ability to create good solutions. Using this formal procedure will help. It may be the shortest distance between a problem and a satisfying solution.

Define the problem, list the causes, think up possible solutions, and pick the best one.

American Reading Ceremony

HAVE YOU EVER WATCHED a Japanese Tea Ceremony? It's really nothing special except for one thing. The person performing the ceremony is *paying attention*. But that one thing makes it extraordinary for both the observers and the performer herself.

Something simple takes place. Someone makes tea and then someone drinks it. But *the spirit in which it is done* makes the difference. Everybody in the room is paying attention and not doing anything else. The person making the tea moves deliberately, unhurried, trying to make each movement perfect.

There's nothing special about tea. Anyone can do the same thing doing just about anything. You can have an American Lunch Ceremony — eat your lunch deliberately, paying attention to what you're doing, unhurried, trying to make each movement in complete awareness.

Try it sometimes when you feel stressed. You can even do it while you work (American Work Ceremony). If you have no immediate deadline, do your work for ten minutes carefully, with your *full attention* on every move, slowly and deliberately. It's a nice little change of pace, if nothing else. But usually there *is* something else, and that's why the Japanese Zen Masters consider the Tea Ceremony as a high art and a worthy practice.

The deliberate movement clarifies your mind and sometimes puts you in a state of tranquility. It often makes you aware that *this moment* is all there is and all that needs to be. It's hard to describe, but you don't need a description. Try it and experience it for yourself. It's nothing mystical. If anything, it is a more down-to-earth experience than our usual hustle and bustle because all you're doing is *paying attention* to what you're doing. Rather than thinking about yesterday's golf game or tonight's dinner, rather than worrying about something that might happen tomorrow or fuming about what happened this morning, rather than wishing you were somewhere else or hoping things change in your future, you're just here, now, doing what you're doing. It is surprising how seldom we do that.

You can do it anywhere, anytime. Try it right now while you're reading. Notice your posture, the sounds in the room, the smells, without trying to change anything. Notice your feelings — your emotional tone, the sensations in your stomach, the feeling of your hands and your forehead...notice the page, the feel of your eyes as they move along the line, the voice in your head saying these words. Just notice.

Thank you for participating with me in this American Reading Ceremony.

Slow down your movements once in awhile and pay attention.

Normally we do not so much look at things as overlook them.

— Alan Watts

Work is Good Therapy

THERAPY CAN BE EXPENSIVE. Work is cheap — they even *pay* you for it! When your work is challenging enough to fully compel your attention, but not so challenging it outstrips your ability, you enter The Enjoyment Zone, where your attention is focused on what you're doing, where you're experiencing the pleasure of being engrossed and engaged in what you're doing, where the petty worries and frustrations that normally plague your mind have no foothold. And whether or not you work in The Enjoyment Zone *is up to you*, not the job. You can *make* your job into an enjoyable pursuit.

If you want to read more about it, read Mihaly Csikszentmihalyi's excellent book, *Flow: The Psychology of Optimal Experience.*

When you can work in that enjoyable state of concentration, you're giving yourself an excellent form of therapy. Work can be therapeutic! It can heal and restore your mind. It can rid you of depression, negative moods, and feelings of helplessness. And it can give you confidence and self-esteem.

One of the things that contributes to negative, unpleasant emotions is *rumination*: dwelling on thoughts you can do nothing about, running negative and self-defeating thoughts through your head over and over, convincing yourself ever more thoroughly of the validity of your misery.

Once these kinds of thoughts get going, they're hard to stop. You feel bad, you think about your situation in a negative way *because* you feel bad, and then the negative way you're thinking makes you feel *worse*. The thoughts are not doing you any good. The best thing you can do is stop thinking about it, but you can't seem to do that. You're like a train on a track, and there is nowhere to go but down.

Engaging work takes your mind off that track. Like distracting a crying baby with a rattle, you send your mind in a new direction.

And while you're working, *you're causing an effect.* Even moving your fingers on a keyboard causes an effect. Helplessness is a core symptom of depression, contributing to it and often causing it. Productive work proves you are *not* helpless, so simply doing your work can lessen or even eliminate a period of depression.

Also, when you work in The Enjoyment Zone, your skills improve. One inevitable consequence of challenging work is an increase in competence and expertise. This gives you confidence and self-esteem — not based merely on the encouraging words of a therapist, but based on real evidence.

Work cannot accomplish everything therapy can, but it can do a great deal of therapeutic good — far more good than leisure (most leisure produces nothing: it doesn't increase skills, competence or self-esteem, and it doesn't engage your mind enough to stop ruminations). Work has, however, been an effective therapy for generations of people. And it can work as well for you.

**Get to work — keep it challenging,
but not stressful.**

THE PEOPLE SECTION

How to Avoid Feeling Socially Awkward

WE'VE ALL FELT IT. You don't know what to say or what to do. You feel too aware of yourself and how you're standing, how you're looking, what you sound like. Teenagers feel it intensely. And some of the things teenagers do that seem so incomprehensible to parents stem from a simple desire to avoid feeling socially awkward.

Although it is *natural* to feel awkward around people you don't know very well, it isn't pleasant or productive. Here are two practical things anyone can do to feel more socially comfortable:

> **1. Relax your muscles.** This makes you calmer. Most people don't have any problem at all being social around people when they're relaxed. That's one of the reasons social gatherings have traditionally served alcoholic drinks: It relaxes people. Relaxation is conducive to sociability. So scan your body and find a muscle that feels tense and consciously relax that muscle. You'll instantly feel more at ease. Your feeling of ease will make you feel less awkward.

2. Make it your mission to help the *other* person feel more comfortable. Make your conversation easy for the other person by asking questions she will enjoy answering. Find out the person's name, whether she's from this area, and if she's not, where she's from. Her answers will probably stimulate other questions and stories. How about her family: Do they live in this area? Does she have a big family? Brothers and sisters? What do they do? How about work? What does she do for a living? Does she like it? What got her into it? How about travel? What parts of the world has she traveled to? Any hobbies? Listen with interest. Let her know you like what she's saying. Help her feel comfortable.

That's six areas to talk about: name, home, family, work, travel, hobbies. Memorize that list of six topics so when you need them, the questions will come to mind easily, keeping your conversation easy and smooth.

A smooth and easy conversation will put the other person at ease, which will make *you* feel more comfortable.

You'll probably never get to all six of the topics because as the other person starts talking, you'll find points of interest and things you have in common that you'll want to know more about, and the two of you will start talking about those, and off you'll go into pleasant conversation. You'll get to know the person and have a wonderful time and you'll forget to feel awkward because you can only feel awkward when you're self-conscious.

As you become increasingly conscious of the other person and conscious of your mission to help her become comfortable, you become less conscious of yourself and your awkwardness disappears.

Relieve your social awkwardness by physically relaxing and concerning yourself with helping the *other* person feel comfortable. And say goodbye forever to feeling awkward in social situations.

Relax your muscles and make it your mission to help the *other* person feel more comfortable.

He who wishes to secure the good of others
has already secured his own.

— *Confucius*

A great deal of my battle, as an actor, is to whittle away the things that make me self-conscious and try to trick myself into not being self-conscious. So, it's always a challenge, whether I'm lying in a hospital bed or flying around with a rocket pack on my back, or what have you. On the best of days, it's a challenge for me.

— *Billy Campbell*

Self-consciousness is hell.

— *Marty Rubin*

How to Be Sincerely Interested

TO BE CLOSER TO PEOPLE, you'll need to become a good listener. And to listen well, the main requirement is to be *sincerely* interested in the other person. The question is, "How can you *become* sincerely interested in someone?"

The answer is: Put yourself in the other's place. Imagine you were her. What would it be like to be her? What would you *feel?* What might you be *thinking?* Do this first and questions start coming easily. Curiosity blossoms into sincere interest.

Normally, I wouldn't care about the plants in someone's yard. I'm not usually interested in that sort of thing. But I was talking to a man yesterday who told me he had taken three truckloads of organic matter out of his back yard. He said he needed to do that before he could start planning how to plant his yard. He just bought his house a little while ago.

I wanted to be sincerely interested, so I imagined I was him. I imagined what it would be like. "That must be fun to have created a kind of blank canvas. Do you know what you're going to plant? Do you have it all planned out?"

When I imagined what it was like for him, I was more interested, more curious — sincerely — than I would have been.

The way to connect, to cultivate closeness, is to be curious about the person — open and curious and *interested.* People open up when you like them and are interested in finding out about them. And the way to be curious is to imagine what that person may be feeling.

Be curious and pay special attention to feelings. When someone utters an expression of feelings, *do not bypass it.* Give it attention. An expression of feelings is the ore you are mining for.

Explore those feelings the same way. What did he feel? *Why* did he feel that way?

When he tells you about something that happened to him, imagine it happened to *you.* How would *you* feel? And then express that. "That must have hurt your feelings." Or, "I think I would have been very relieved."

Don't presume you know what he felt, because you don't really know. But open it up, invite him to talk about it. Tell him what you guess he might be feeling and let him confirm it or elaborate or correct you.

Imagine being the other person — that's the key to becoming sincerely interested.

Imagine you were the other person and ask the questions that come to mind.

If there is any one secret of success, it lies in the ability to get the other person's point of view and see things from that person's angle as well as from your own.

— *Henry Ford*

Your Inner Guide to Self-Esteem

SELF-ESTEEM HAS BEEN A HOT TOPIC for years. And for a good reason: Low self-esteem is a source of trouble — bad marriages, social isolation, violence, lack of success, depression, conflict in the workplace, etc. Low self-esteem causes problems. The obvious solution is to try to improve people's self-esteem by pointing out their good traits. Psychologists told us we could give our children high self-esteem by complimenting and praising them often. And they said you could protect yourself by making an effort to think well of yourself — to say good things to yourself, repeat affirmations, make a point of acknowledging your good traits, etc.

Recent research at Wake Forest University might be turning that popular philosophy completely upside down. The funny thing is, when all the smoke has cleared, what we've got left bears a remarkable resemblance to simple common sense.

According to the research, self-esteem appears to be an internal guide to how well we're doing socially, somewhat like our internal guide to the temperature.

Usually, when you feel hot, you take off some clothing or open a window. And when you feel cold, you bundle up. Although you might be able to repeat to yourself over and over "I feel warm, I feel warm," there are better things to do with your time. Might as well just put on a sweater and get on with it. It's useful to have an internal guide — a feeling — that lets you know what's happening in the world around you, and gives you some motivation to do something about it.

Apparently, that's exactly what self-esteem is.

The feeling of low self-esteem is apparently nothing more than an indication you aren't getting enough positive feedback from other people. You may not be getting rejected or criticized, but to really feel good about ourselves, we need something more than that. We need acknowledgment, compliments, appreciation. We need people to notice us and like us.

This is where it gets tricky. As a parent, you might want to improve your child's self-esteem by giving him lots of compliments. But watch out. If you exaggerate your acknowledgments or if you sometimes make a big deal out of a small thing or resort to puffery, you may be setting your child's internal gauge "off the beam." You've set his social-status meter too high, and it no longer measures the situation accurately. Your child then grows up and goes out into the world and has difficulty dealing with people.

Some research at Northeastern University showed that people who think a lot of themselves — regardless of how others feel about them — tend to be perceived by others as condescending and hostile.

Given this new information, a different approach to creating self-esteem seems in order: Giving honest and *accurate* feedback to our children, our spouses, and our employees. It is easy to compliment and praise people. It makes *them* feel good, and it makes *us* feel good to make them feel good. It's more difficult to find something you genuinely appreciate and to say it without the slightest bit of puffery, but it just might do more good.

We can also help people *do better*. Of course! If someone is getting along well with her peers and she's succeeding at something — trumpet, hobby, volunteer work, schoolwork, job, athletics — it will improve her self-esteem. So find a way to help her *accomplish* something. When people do well, they tend to feel better about themselves.

When you want to build *your own* self-esteem, it appears your best bet is to change your *behavior*. Do your tasks well and treat people well and you'll feel good about yourself. Don't worry so much about how you *think* about yourself. Change what you *do* to make yourself more appreciated by the people around you. Increase your value to other people and to the company you work for.

Watch the reactions of other people. Pay attention to the reality outside your skin. Do more of what works. Do less of what doesn't get the response you want. Your self-esteem, your internal "sociometer" will rise as an accurate reflection of your true abilities and where you stand with the people in your life.

To improve the self-esteem of others:
Give unexaggerated feedback and help them gain ability.

To improve your own self-esteem:
Change what you do to make yourself more appreciated by the people around you.

Truth is a deep kindness.

— Kahlil Gibran

Change People Without Criticizing

IN DALE CARNEGIE'S BOOK, *How to Win Friends and Influence People*, the first principle is, "Don't criticize, condemn or complain." But that rule seems impossible to follow, doesn't it? We *need* to criticize sometimes because people can fool themselves about their shortcomings, and some simply don't know any better.

Living and working with other people requires that you criticize occasionally.

But almost everyone dislikes criticism. It can evoke negative feelings of tension, resentment, and hurt feelings. And if you do it *poorly*, a criticism (and the defensive response people often make to it) can solidify and fortify the very thing you're trying to change, making it virtually impossible for the person to change it in the future, because in response to a criticism, people sometimes justify what they did, reinforcing their commitment to it.

This is a tough situation. But you can soften or eliminate many of the dangers of criticizing with a simple method. It doesn't come naturally (you need to practice the method to do it well) but it is a way to criticize without creating hard feelings. It is a way to help people change for the better. It will allow you to have a more positive impact on the people you live and work with, and helps you avoid adding more tension and anxiety to your life.

What seems impossible — never criticizing — becomes possible when you change the criticism into a *request* before it leaves your mouth. You don't have to say anything about a mistake the person made. That's now in the past. Don't tell them they're wrong or need to get their ears cleaned or whatever. Simply request what you want in the *future.*

A bad criticism might go something like this: "You never pay attention. I have told you this at least a hundred times! I hate it when you throw your jacket on the floor. Quit being such a slob!" That's not the most effective way to deliver a criticism. It probably won't get you the result you want. It destroys feelings of affection. Changed to a request, it'll sound more like this: "Would you please do me a favor and hang up your jacket?"

What do you think? If you were on the receiving end, would you have a different experience? Which would you like better? Me too. So turn your complaints into requests.

It still isn't the most fun thing to do, but modifying a criticism into a request takes some of the discomfort out of it *for both of you.* And admitting *you* aren't perfect makes it even *easier* to hear. (It also improves your own state. It keeps you from feeling and coming across as "holier-than-thou.")

"But I've already said it as a request *several* times," one woman said to me, "I've done what you're suggesting and it doesn't work."

"Have you ever tried to change a habit?" I asked her.

"Of course I have," she replied, wondering what that has to do with anything.

"Tell me about a habit you changed successfully."

She thought about it for a few seconds and said, "I used to bite my fingernails when I was younger."

"That's a good one," I said, "Now tell me: After you made the decision to stop biting your fingernails, did your habit disappear immediately?"

"No. But I..."

"Of course not," I interrupted, "because habits don't disappear that easily. You probably tried and failed several times before you finally succeeded."

"Yes, but…"

I was on a roll, so I interrupted the poor woman again, "Now think about this: You want your husband to call you when he's going to be late because you don't like to worry, and you have successfully converted your criticisms into requests — congratulations and good work, by the way — but he *still* doesn't call you."

"Well, he did the time before last. But he didn't last night."

"This is how habits are *formed!*" I said, practically yelling at her, "first you decide to change something. An opportunity to put your decision into practice comes and goes and you completely forget — your new decision doesn't occur to you until afterwards. You make up your mind you'll remember *next* time, and you fail again. And maybe again and again. But if you keep trying, one day it will occur to you *in time* to apply the new habit. You may miss the next opportunity or two, but if you keep trying, eventually you can form a new habit."

"Okay, I get it," she says, "I need to give him time to form the habit. I guess I can do that."

"It's not going to be that easy," I said. "It is not *his* habit he is trying to change. It is his habit *you* are trying to change, and if you want to be successful, you'll have to take responsibility to remind him *over and over* — lovingly, patiently, with a full understanding of how difficult it is to change a habit. If you can do this and persist, he will change his habit, if he loves you."

"He loves me," she said quietly. "This is good. I guess I never really thought of it that way. But I'm pretty sure if

I do it like you said, he would change. He'd do anything for me."

She did do it, and she was right — he changed. She turned her criticism into a *request* and asked it *with affection* again and again. It worked so well because she didn't criticize or condemn him.

This is just as effective at work. Daniel Isenberg, a researcher at the Harvard Business School, studied the differences between successful and unsuccessful executives. He found the old stereotypes weren't true. The successful executives were not impatient, arrogant, or insensitive. As Lewis Andrews wrote:

> "Isenberg has found the most successful senior managers are quite extraordinary in their ability to refrain from overt criticism of others, often humorously conceding when they themselves are wrong. They also take a greater than normal interest in the emotional comfort of their fellow workers and have a tendency to transform everyday resentments over unexpected problems into constructive questions about how to improve their company's operations."

I used to have a natural tendency to be too blunt when I criticized people. I didn't like to criticize, so I tried to get it over with as quickly as possible. I knew it didn't work, but it was a habit. I decided to change it.

My wife, Klassy, gives a lot of public speeches and one night I was sitting in on one of her presentations. There are two important facts about criticizing, and she was explaining them. The first is that it helps to "sandwich" a criticism between two positive statements, and the second is that it works better to ask for what you *want* in the *future* rather than criticize what has already happened. She encapsulated them into this short phrase: *Make 'em right, make a request, make 'em right.*

I thought to myself, "That's it!" That's a short, easy-to-remember phrase that says the whole idea. It even has a nice rhythm to it. I started to repeat the phrase often, and it became part of my thinking habits — it started coming into my mind by itself.

One night I was writing a note to my son and I wrote a command and a criticism. Then the thought occurred to me: Make him right, make a (polite) request, make him right. I threw away the old note and wrote a new one. It said the same thing as the old one, but in a different way — a way that would inspire *cooperation* instead of grudging compliance and resentment.

A researcher at the University of Washington, John Gottman, PhD, found that the difference between a request and a criticism is crucial to the longevity and happiness of a marriage. Criticism is about the past, and is usually an attack on the *person*. A request centers on *behavior* in the *future*. That little difference makes a big difference.

As Gottman has discovered, requests for change are one of the healthiest things you can do for your marriage. Criticism, and the mutual contempt that can evolve out of it, is the most destructive. It causes resentment. It makes people unable to talk to each other. People can forget why they ever fell in love in the first place.

Criticism doesn't usually go anywhere. "You're so selfish!" When someone says that to you, what can you do? Become less selfish? What does that even mean? But how much easier it is to respond to the request: "If you're going to be more than twenty minutes late, please call me and let me know."

When someone says that to you, what can you do? Well, you can do it, or you can say, "How about later than thirty minutes," or whatever. But the point is, you can *do* something about it other than just feel bad. And that's what's important: It minimizes the negativity. It's more efficient. And you will have the pleasure of enjoying more affection.

There is no way you're going to be able to live with someone without disliking some things. No two people are perfectly compatible. We're all different, and if you put any two of us together for awhile, some things are going to start rubbing us the wrong way. But we can compromise. We can bargain. We can communicate, and by doing so, we can *minimize* the unhappiness and *maximize* the pleasure of being together.

Instead of criticizing, make a request.

If someone takes awhile to change, remind them, with kindness, again and again.

Criticism, like rain, should be gentle enough to nourish a man's growth without destroying his roots.

— Frank A. Clark

Here Comes the Judge

YOU ARE KIND AND GENEROUS most of the time. But occasionally you judge, label and disapprove of people — sometimes silently in your mind, sometimes you speak it out loud, sometimes you do it for significant reasons, sometimes you do it for petty reasons.

Judging people causes an underlying resentment that puts you in a bad mood and makes you tired. And it can put a strain on your relationships with people. The stresses from different sources in your life compound your suffering, and this is a source you can do without.

And no matter how you do it or what the circumstances, when you pass judgment on someone, you are very likely making an error — usually committing at least one of these three forms of what cognitive scientists call "distorted thinking:"

1. Jumping to conclusions. We rarely know the motives or full story behind the actions a person takes, and yet we come to conclusions quickly and easily that "he's a jerk" or "she's a fool" or "how rude" or "what a freak." We condemn people far too easily.

2. Overgeneralization. A judgment normally involves summing up a complex human being in simple terms based on a few or even one instance. That's poor science and faulty thinking.

3. Overconfidence in one's own assessment. You don't really know *why* other people do things. And yet you hold your judgments with excessive confidence. We all do it. Overconfidence in our conclusions is a fallibility of human nature.

These thought-mistakes can be corrected with practice. The technique is simple: Pay attention to your assessments of other people, and then *question and criticize* your judgments. Are you jumping to conclusions? Are you overgeneralizing? Do you have enough knowledge to be able to make such an assessment?

Think about it as rationally as you can. Maybe you're being too hasty. Maybe you're being unnecessarily harsh. Haven't you yourself done something similar? Sure you have. But there were extenuating circumstances that at least partially excused you, weren't there? Maybe this person has reasons too, but you don't know about them. It's not only possible, it's very likely.

Question your judgments and you'll find that many of them aren't worth much, and you'll stop holding them.

And what will happen? You'll feel less stress. You will find your relationships gently blossoming in a new way. You'll be able to talk to the person more freely. You'll be more relaxed. Conflicts will be easier to resolve because you'll be able to communicate without anger (no judgment, no anger) and without making the other person defensive (when you're not judging, people don't feel attacked, so they don't get defensive).

And in the long run, less stress, anger, and frustration adds up to better health too.

Once you start paying attention to it, you may find out you're in the habit of judging people a lot. Does this make you bad and wrong? No. Only human. Judging *yourself* is faulty thinking too.

Question and criticize your negative judgments of people.

If we could read the secret history of our enemies, we should find in each man's life sorrow and suffering enough to disarm all hostility.

— Henry Wadsworth Longfellow

Beware, so long as you live, of judging men by their outward appearance.

— Jean de La Fontaine

The least amount of judging we can do, the better off we are.

— Michael J. Fox

Confidence With People

WITH CONFIDENCE you're more attractive and likable, and you feel better than when you lack confidence. You've experienced the truth of that statement many times in your life. But isn't confidence something you either have or don't, something you're either born with or not? Can you deliberately *become* confident?

I'm confident you can.

You see, if we just use a synonym for *confident*, the way becomes obvious. One of its synonyms is "certain." And it is true that you feel confident wherever you have a lot of certainty.

Think about it. For a teenage boy who wants to talk to a girl he likes, he may feel very awkward and not confident at all. But if he knew a lot about computers, and she was having a problem with a computer and asked his help, he could help her and feel confident doing so.

Why?

Because he would know what he was talking about. People feel confident when they are certain.

Therefore, wherever *you* would like to feel confident, develop more certainty about it. And I don't mean an *attitude* of certainty; I mean develop real honest-to-goodness, *actual* certainty.

If, for example, you have to get up and speak to a group next week and you don't feel confident about it, start working to develop some degree of certainty: Talk to the people you need to talk to and find out who will be there and what they are expecting, and then prepare thoroughly.

The more you prepare, rehearse, talk about what you will say to your friends, make notes, do research, the more certain you will be and the more confident you will feel.

As another example, a shy person might feel a lack of confidence meeting new people. When she's introduced to someone, she doesn't like it, feels awkward, and feels like withdrawing. This is a common experience, even in people who aren't very shy.

But why would this be so?

Because a new person is — by definition — *unknown.* Our shy person is not certain about anything except the person's name (and if she is too distracted by her nervousness, she'll quickly lose her certainty about that too).

But surprisingly, even with a person you've never met before, you can know with certainty quite a bit about him. And our shy person can increase her certainty and therefore her confidence when dealing with people by:

1. Learning more about the human nature we all have in common.

2. Learning more about manners (so you're certain about what should be done when).

3. Learning strategies for getting to know someone.

You can learn human nature and customs and manners and strategies so well you have a high degree of certainty about those things.

This would add up to more confidence around people — even people you've never met before. A good book to start with is Dale Carnegie's *How to Win Friends and Influence People.* It is basic information about the fundamental aspects of the human nature we all have in common, and how to treat people so they feel well-treated.

There are many ways to gain certainty about people, and each one increases your feeling of confidence a little more.

Confidence is not on or off; there are many shades of gray from No Confidence to Absolute Confidence. Any actions you take to increase your level of certainty slides you over a little more toward confidence.

Increase your certainty about how to act.

Smile, for everyone lacks self-confidence and more than any other one thing a smile reassures them.

— Andre Maurois

There are two types of people — those who come into a room and say, "Well, here I am!" and those who come in and say, "Ah, there you are."

— Frederick Collins

Break Out

IN LEWIS ANDREWS' excellent book, *To Thine Own Self Be True*, he writes, "To the extent we compromise our integrity to make an attractive image of ourselves, we lose contact with our natural enthusiasm. We become contrived, artificial...bored."

I thought that was somewhat interesting when I first read it, and then I went on about my business.

But one day I figured out how it works and what it had to do with *me*. Trying to make an attractive image of myself is not as unusual or rare as I originally thought. I do it a lot. And so do you.

People expect you to be something in particular, and you expect yourself to act a certain way also — often. The trouble with that is: It leaves you with no flexibility, no freedom, and thus no enthusiasm for living.

People used to comment on my attitude — I was so cheerful and full of life. After *Self-Help Stuff That Works* was first published, people began to expect me to be in a great mood all the time. After all, I wrote a book on how to improve your own attitude.

I did not want to disappoint them. I wanted them to think well of me and my book. I wanted to prove the principles were good. But every moment I spent trying to live up to an image ruined my attitude. It sapped my enthusiasm. It was stressful and it made me resentful of those people for their unrealistic expectations of me.

That's when Andrews' message hit home. When you try to live up to an image, he said, it kills your natural enthusiasm for living.

After I realized that, I deliberately started doing what I wanted, and had the determination to make sure I didn't do anything to live up to someone else's expectations.

And you know what? I was in a great mood. That very day, for the first time in a long time, someone commented on my great attitude.

Opera singer Rise Stevens had a lot of poise and confidence on stage, but she was not comfortable hanging around with others. "My discomfort came from trying to be something I was not," she said, "a star in the drawing room as well as on stage. If a clever person made a joke, I tried to top it — and failed. I pretended to be familiar with subjects I knew nothing of..."

But then she had a personal revelation. She says, "I realized that I simply wasn't a wit or an intellectual and that I could succeed only as myself. I began listening and asking questions at parties instead of trying to impress the guests. When I spoke, I tried to contribute, not to shine. Almost at once I started feeling new warmth in my social contacts. They liked the real me better."

Whenever you feel yourself harden into a fixed persona, *break out!* Whenever you lack natural enthusiasm for living, find out where you're trying to live up to someone's expectation and break out of it. Start creating your life again right from that point, as an artist would take down a painted canvas and put up a new blank one.

The price you will pay is that you will, in fact, disappoint some people. And you will always have the choice: Live up to someone's expectations *or* have a natural enthusiasm for living.

Choose one and then the other for awhile, just to get a feel for the difference in results. Eventually you'll settle on freeing yourself from trying to live up to an image and you'll relax and be yourself.

Don't try to live up to an image.

I must be myself. I will not hide my tastes or aversions. I will so trust that what is deep is holy, that I will do strongly before the sun and moon whatever inly rejoices me and the heart appoints.

— Ralph Waldo Emerson

The hardest thing about being in this business is just being able to be yourself. People act like there's this one set of rules to follow to be a pop star and I think, "Well, you say I'm a pop star, so maybe that's not true."

— Kelly Clarkson

Always be yourself, express yourself, have faith in yourself, do not go out and look for a successful personality and duplicate it.

— Bruce Lee

A Friend in Deed

IT OFTEN HELPS A FRIEND to listen to him talk when he's having troubles. But being the listener isn't easy, and as you know, not everything you say or do to help a distressed person really helps. Brant Burleson, a researcher at Purdue University, set up some experiments to find out just what *does* help, and what doesn't. What he discovered may surprise you, because the most helpful things are the *easiest* things, although they may feel unnatural.

You don't have to offer advice. In fact, you probably shouldn't, according to Burleson's studies. When someone is unloading his troubles, most of the things we most naturally want to do will not help him.

For example, it doesn't help much to tell your friend about similar troubles you've had, or to try to help him look on the bright side, or to try to change the subject.

What actually helps the listener is surprisingly simple and easy:

> Encourage your friend to describe his trouble *in great detail.* And make sure your friend includes, as part of that detail, descriptions of your friend's *feelings.*

That's it. Most people can pretty much figure out what they ought to do once they think about it, and that's exactly what you're allowing them to do: Think.

By not giving your friend advice or trying to help her see the silver lining, by not cluttering her mind with your own similar experiences, and by getting her to describe her feelings and the problem in detail, you're allowing her to clarify the situation for herself, to sort out what happened and how she feels and to figure out how she should think about it and what she should do.

It's easier to think by speaking aloud than it is to try to think to yourself, especially when you're upset, but that's true *only* if the listener is allowing you to speak freely.

Get your friend to describe her problem and her feelings *in detail.*

Although it may seem you're hardly doing anything, you're giving her what she needs most when times are tough: A friend to confide in.

Encourage your friend to describe her trouble in great detail.

Listening is a magnetic and strange thing, a creative force. The friends who listen to us are the ones we move toward. When we are listened to, it creates us, makes us unfold and expand.

— *Karl A. Menninger*

Attitudes and Kin

OUR MOODS HAVE a significant impact on our health and our ability to make sound decisions. When something consistently alters your mood for the worse, it's bad for you. And whatever puts *you* in a bad mood is bad for your friends, your significant other, and bad for your kids (if you have them), because *your moods are contagious.*

The bad moods of many people are often caused by one of their relatives — Mom, Dad, a brother or sister, an in-law. The trouble is, we tend to put up with lousy behavior from a relative — behavior we would *never* tolerate in our spouse or children or in our friends. We don't speak up. We feel that we *have to* put up with it because they are "family." But we don't.

There is no law that says you have to stay on good terms with a person just because he's a relative. You don't. And trying to stay on good terms might bring you down and, by contagion, put your friends, your significant other, and your children in a bad mood often enough to impact their health and their ability to get along with others.

It's only a matter of luck whether your relatives can also be your friends. If you didn't get lucky, don't worry about it. You have your loved ones to look out for. And there are plenty of people other than your relatives you can have relationships with — people who will treat you well.

Should you write off a relative who brings you down? No. There's a better way. Simply follow these two rules:

1. Be honest
2. Don't judge

These two rules will help you clean up a relationship. Those who bring you down will tend to gradually remove themselves *voluntarily* from your life.

The truth is, when someone brings us down *regularly*, we are collaborating in the process by withholding honest statements. For example: "Would you please call me later? I'm busy right now." We don't say stuff like that because we're trying to be polite. We don't want to be rude. But whatever the reason we have for withholding honest communication, hiding the truth only digs us deeper into the mess.

The way out of this mess is with straightforward information, such as the following: "I don't really feel we should talk about him behind his back." "That question makes me uncomfortable." "I don't want you to visit." "I think you drink too much and I don't want my kids to be around it." Simple, honest communication is all you need.

Some honest statements may seem *unnecessarily* harsh. But those are the kind of things you need to say sometimes if you want to protect your psychological and physical health and that of your loved ones. The problem is we sometimes don't have enough courage to say those things until we are really mad. They seem so harsh, you'd think you'd have to be angry to say them. But you don't. You don't even have to think the person is wrong. In fact, that's the other half it: Restrain yourself from judging the person. If you judge your relative and make him wrong, you hurt him and yourself, and that's unnecessary. You can speak honestly without judgment. It may take some practice, but you can do it. Concentrate on it. Memorize those two rules. Chant them to yourself when you're visiting with the person or talking to them over the phone. Be honest gently, without judgment.

So the way to deal with a relative who puts you in a bad mood is to let him be the way he is while also taking care of yourself by being honest. Remind yourself that if you had similar upbringing and genetics, you might very well be like him, so there's no justification for writing him off as a bad person. You don't know how he came to be that way and you don't know his motives. All you really know is he brings *you* down.

Concern yourself with being honest — *without judgment* — and the honesty will take care of your situation for you. Your relative will either respond to your honesty well and your relationship will improve, or he won't like your honesty — he won't want to be around you — and he will voluntarily phase *you* out of *his* life. Either way, you're better off. It may be a little rough for awhile, but you and your loved ones will come out on the other side healthier and happier.

Clean up relationships by being honest without judgment.

The truth that many people never understand, until it is too late, is that the more you try to avoid suffering the more you suffer because smaller things begin to torture you in proportion to your fear of suffering.

— Thomas Merton

Very Impressive

I REMEMBER READING about an ingenious experiment showing how hard it is to change people's minds after they've already formed an opinion. Check this out.

The researchers took people who believed in the death penalty and people who didn't, and showed them studies on the subject. Some studies were comparisons between two states of the U.S. — one with the death penalty and one without — and how their crime rates differed. Other studies showed "before and after" crime rates of states that either did or did not have the death penalty and then changed their policies.

The experimenters discovered that *no matter which* of the studies they showed people, their opinions did not change!

Not only that, but whether they were for or against the death penalty, these people, all of whom viewed the same studies, became *even more convinced* of their original opinion. To all of them, the studies only reinforced their already existing opinions.

What they did was find flaws — legitimate in most cases — in the studies, which gave them good reasons *not* to change their opinion.

But they only criticized the study that did *not* support their opinion and they praised the study that did, pointing out all the (again, legitimate) reasons the study was a good one.

But nobody changed their opinion.

This probably doesn't surprise you. Most of us realize that people don't like to change their opinions, and that they skew their perception of events to support their own opinions, and tend to criticize or be skeptical of unsupportive events.

Now here's the point: People also do that with their opinions of *you.*

When you first meet someone, they size you up and form an opinion about you. If you are cranky the first time you meet someone, they will tend to think of you as a grumpy person. If you are not grumpy the next time they see you, they usually won't think to themselves, "Oh, I was mistaken." They will think to themselves, "Oh, Mister Grumpy is pretending to be nice today." They will discount it if what you're doing now is inconsistent with their first impression of you.

That's why it often takes a long time to change someone's first impression — and why it's important to make a good one when you have a chance.

Try to make a good first impression.

Early impressions are hard to eradicate from the mind. When once wool has been dyed purple, who can restore it to its previous whiteness?

— *Saint Jerome*

Danger

I USED TO THINK it was healthy to express anger and unhealthy to hold it in, so I said what was on my mind when I was angry. Of course, I hurt people's feelings — unnecessarily.

Anger can be a dangerous and destructive emotion. Although you can't eliminate the emotion from your life, the way you respond to it can make it less dangerous and more constructive.

Research has shown that *expressing* the emotion of anger usually just makes you angrier. But that doesn't mean you should avoid saying anything about what makes you angry. It's just that you should avoid saying it *while you are angry*. It doesn't do much good anyway: The person listening to you only sees and hears your anger and puts up her defenses right away. Not much gets through. And your listener gets a bad impression of you. You might also say things you will regret later.

But since you feel angry, you probably need to say *something*. Follow these two rules and you stand a good chance of being effective:

> 1. Make it your personal policy not to say much or decide anything while you're angry. Leave it alone, go on about your business, and the intensity will subside. *Then* think about what you need to do or say or decide. If you've calmed down and decided to talk to someone but find you can't

seem to say it without getting angry, write it in a letter.

2. *Say what you want*, not what you *don't* want. Say your complaints in the form of requests. Instead of "You never do such and such," say "Would you please do such and such?" It's easier to hear. It's more likely to cause the effect you want. Say clearly what you want and why you want it.

Usually you're angry because you want someone to change — to do something different than what they're doing. That's perfectly legitimate. What you want is to have an impact on the other, which, according to the research, is what will really and truly make your anger disappear. Not venting, but not remaining silent either.

Those two steps will help you effectively cause change in other people while reducing the amount of anger you experience over time. Even when you make a request and someone says no, you will feel better. At least now they know what you want. You've said it. It's off your chest.

This is a good way to increase others' respect for you while also making things go the way you want more often. Turn your complaints into requests and make those requests when you are calm.

Don't say much when you're angry.

When you complain, say what you want, not what you don't want.

How to Find a Lifemate

IN ORDER TO FIND A LOVE FOR LIFE, you'll need to know what your strongest interest is. What really *interests* you? What do you love to talk about, read about, do, have, play with? If you don't know the answer to those questions, or if the answers are a bunch of minor interests rather than one major interest, forget about finding a mate until you know what your "passion" is. But once you know, finding a mate is easy: *Pursue your interest* and see who shows up.

Let's say you love sailing. If you want to find someone you'll love to talk to, you'll need to find someone as interested in sailing as you are. Otherwise, although the two of you may have a functional relationship, you'll be living in different worlds. Our deepest purposes and interests are at the heart of who we are.

So join a sailing club, go to sailing classes and races. Pursue your interest. The people you meet in a sailing club are *much* more likely to be interested in sailing than the people you'd meet in a bar, for example.

The rush of hormones at the beginning of a relationship wears off. No matter how attractive someone may be, that initial intense rush eventually dies down. But that's okay, because there's a deeper, more satisfying kind of love and it fuels attraction: The respect and affection between two people who share a common purpose or interest.

Raising children ends up being the common purpose between many married couples. But if child raising doesn't intensely interest both of you, it isn't a good enough purpose to create and maintain happiness.

Two things need to be said. First, you'll never find the "perfect" mate. She or he may seem perfect for a while, but no one can meet all of your ideals. In fact, some of your ideals are probably mutually exclusive, so meeting all of them is literally impossible. You'll eventually find faults in anyone because everyone has faults. When you find faults with your mate, remind yourself of that. Quit imagining that there is a perfect person out there somewhere. There isn't.

Second, even when you've found your lifemate, you'll sometimes be attracted to others. It's human. It doesn't mean anything except that you are a biological machine, built to breed. The human species (and every other species on the planet) has a built-in urge to multiply. Stick with your mate and don't let it be important that others sometimes attract you. Your response to yourself can simply be "So what if I'm attracted to someone? It doesn't mean anything."

Stay true to your mate even when an occasional attraction tempts you to do otherwise. You'll be happier and healthier as a result.

You want to find a lifemate? Take up your strongest interest with enthusiasm and see who shows up. After you find the person you're looking for and the rush of hormones has worn off, accept the fact that your mate isn't perfect, that nobody is perfect, and remind yourself that it isn't important that you're occasionally attracted to others. Do this and you can live (pretty darn) happily ever after.

Pursue your interest and remind yourself: Nobody's perfect and attraction to others is unimportant.

Personal Propaganda

WHEN THE EXPERTS want to change the way people think, they use slogans. Why?

Because it works.

Since early in the last century, observers have pointed out that propaganda campaigns have the tendency to use short, easy-to-remember phrases that can encapsulate and symbolize their message. These brief phrases are then repeated over and over again until their meaning becomes part of the thinking habits of the population.

Advertisers do the same thing — *it's the real thing, just do it, finger lickin good, think outside the bun, melts in your mouth, not in your hands, this Bud's for you* — short, pithy, memorable phrases take advantage of the way the human mind works naturally. It's practical. The short phrases focus the mind, simplify the issue and stimulate action.

Our minds don't handle complicated formulas or doctrines very well unless we concentrate our attention. That's fine when we're reading or listening to a lecture. But when it comes down to our daily experiences — when we're late for work, and we're trying to remember where we left the car keys — we find it distinctly difficult to concentrate our occupied minds on any complicated concept, no matter how beautiful or perfect the concept seemed to be when we read it.

In the heat of everyday life, we need to focus on what is happening. We don't have extra attention to spend philosophizing about it.

That's true for everyone: rich or poor, genius or average, in free countries and in communist countries. That is just how the human brain works.

When a ruthless dictator uses short phrases to focus ideas and make them easier to act upon, it may be bad for the people. But you can use the *same* tool to produce some good for yourself. You, too, can take advantage of the way your mind works.

When there's something you want to change about yourself — some habit, some way you deal with others — think it through and then encapsulate your conclusions into a short, easy-to-remember phrase. Say that phrase to yourself often. Use it to focus your mind. Use the phrase to direct your thoughts. Use it to channel your actions in the direction you want.

The source of most of the habits you want to change are habits of *thought*. Change the thought habits and your behavioral habits change too.

For example, when I feel out of my element or if I'm dealing with a task that feels too big for me, I often use the principle from the chapter, *Adrift*. I tell myself: "I can handle it."

With those four words, I remind myself of the simple truth that others have been through worse, and it immediately puts my situation in perspective.

Slogans can really help at times like those — times when you are too busy or too emotional or too overwhelmed to do much thinking about it. Say the slogan to yourself and get right back on track in a good frame of mind without skipping a beat.

Make your own propaganda campaign in your head. Use some of the principles of this book, or encapsulate a change you want or an insight you've had into a short phrase and repeat it often.

Encapsulate and repeat. Encapsulate and repeat. It's a practical technique for improving your life.

Encapsulate your insights into short phrases and repeat them often.

No steam or gas drives anything until it is confined. No life ever grows great until it is focused, dedicated, disciplined.

— Harry Emerson Fosdick

Repetition of the same thought or physical action develops into a habit which, repeated frequently enough, becomes an automatic reflex.

— Norman Vincent Peale

It's the repetition of affirmations that leads to belief. And once that belief becomes a deep conviction, things begin to happen.

— Muhammad Ali

Play Yourself Down

WHEN YOU HEAR SOMEONE bragging or thinking they're better than you, what's your first instinct? To take them down a notch? Let them know they're not as great as they think they are? And when someone is humble or playing themselves down, what do you want to do? Build them up, probably. It's human nature.

The problem is, when you do well — even if you aren't an egotist or a braggart — some people can get the impression you think you're pretty hot stuff, and they'll try to tear you down.

Therefore — and here's the point — if you get more criticism than you want, *play yourself down.* Get to it before they do.

If you play yourself down well enough and quickly enough, the criticizer may even do a complete turnaround and try to build you up. At least they'll have less desire to tear you down. You've taken the wind out of their sails by playing *yourself* down.

There are rules to playing yourself down. You can't just go around saying, "I am nothing. I'm worthless. I'm navel lint." Too obvious. Here are a few pointers:

1. Never lie. Not only does lying feel bad, but if the other person knows or suspects you're lying, it reverses the effect you're trying to create.

2. Don't make a big deal about it. Don't go on and on about how imperfect you are: It'll sound

like you're trying to convince yourself. Just make a brief comment and go on.

3. Point out something the other person is better at than you. Often people who make a habit of tearing other people down feel intensely competitive, and it'll help them relax to feel like a winner.

4. Never mention you're better at something than the other person unless it's absolutely necessary. This will only be difficult if you yourself are intensely competitive.

5. When you make a mistake, admit it before anyone else can accuse you. This is a good thing to do anyway, but it also helps keep people from trying to tear you down.

It sounds contradictory, but people admire humility — as long as it is humility with class. Follow these guidelines and you'll achieve just that. The end result will be a more peaceful, less contentious, happier life.

Play yourself down.

It is far more impressive when others discover your good qualities without your help.

— Judith Martin

The Conflict of Honesty

WE'RE AFRAID TO BE HONEST. I'll admit it, I am too. And we *should* be afraid of it. Honesty can cause conflict — uncomfortable, gut-wrenching, upsetting confrontations with people. We hate those and try to avoid them. One of the main reasons we try to avoid conflict is because we're not very good at it. And because we avoid it, we never have a *chance* to become good at it.

Luckily, many people have gone before you. Some of them have risked honesty and became competent at dealing with the conflict honesty can create, and some of them have even written down what they've learned. Many a wise person has come before us and left behind their hard-earned wisdom.

It seems that there are some basic rules you can follow, and with a little practice, you can learn to deal with conflict in a way that helps other people and yourself at the same time. Here are the two main rules to follow when you find yourself in conflict with someone:

1. Listen well. Interruptions block the flow of communication and prevent progress. Sometimes an interruption jars or upsets the speaker. Give people your attention. Let them finish. Do your best to understand what they're saying. You don't have to *agree* with what they're saying, but try to understand it from their point of view — try to understand why they think that way. And *let them know* you understand.

2. Speak only what's strictly true. This sounds a lot easier than it is. Try it. Try going a day only saying what you *know* is true. I'm not talking about abstract philosophical stuff, either; I don't mean getting into a debate about whether or not your chair really exists. I mean, in a *practical* sense, see if you can go a whole day *only* saying what you know is true. It's tougher than you'd think, so don't treat this one lightly. During conflict, concentrate on saying only what you *know* is true.

Impose these two disciplines on yourself. You will be able to be more honest and you'll have more control over your life. This is no small accomplishment. Honesty sounds kind of corny, but more honesty means more freedom and more personal strength. And no lasting peace can settle in your heart without it.

Be honest. If it causes conflict, listen well and only say what is strictly true.

Between them whom there is hearty truth,
there is love.

— Henry David Thoreau

Bond of Comrades

HAVE YOU EVER SEEN the movie, *Rudy?* It's the true story of a young man who has one all-time dream — to play football for Notre Dame. He has dreamed of it since he was a little kid. When Rudy is a young adult, he is working in a mill with his best friend, Pete. They've been best friends since childhood. In one scene, it is Rudy's birthday, and Pete gives him a Notre Dame letterman's jacket. Rudy immediately tries it on and looks at Pete. "This is fantastic," says Rudy, "Pete, where did you find this?"

"I was in Gary and I saw it in this surplus store," says Pete, "and I said, 'That's gotta be yours!'"

Rudy is obviously affected by having a tangible representation of his dream. "This is unbelievable." He puts the jacket on. "Pete, I don't know how I'm ever going to thank you…How's it look?" Pete looks him in the eye and says with full conviction, "You were *born* to wear that jacket."

Rudy had always wanted to play for Notre Dame, but he wasn't very big and he wasn't very fast. He didn't have much athletic ability. He also had dyslexia (which he didn't know yet), so he had difficulty with his schoolwork and got bad grades in high school. And his family didn't have the money to send him to college. To all outward appearances, he didn't have a chance of ever even *attending* Notre Dame, much less playing on their football team.

Rudy looks at his jacket. Then he looks at Pete and says, "You're the only one who ever took me serious, Pete."

It is a moving scene and an excellent demonstration of a bond between comrades.

If you think about it, the bond of deep friendship between two people is really what makes life truly meaningful. When people think their life is about to end, almost everyone has the same thought. It's not about money or problems or who is right and who is wrong; it's not about politics or philosophy. All is stripped away except the single most important value, the one that made this trip worth the trouble. Friendship.

Viktor Frankl wrote about an experience he'd had while he was in one of Hitler's concentration camps. One morning as he was marching through the snow — starving, severely abused, not knowing if or when he would ever see a normal life, he thought of his wife. He did not even know if she was still alive. But in his mind's eye, he saw her, and she smiled at him. Powerful feelings washed over him. He later wrote about this experience:

> "For the first time in my life I saw the truth as it is set into song by so many poets, proclaimed as the final wisdom by so many thinkers. The truth — that love is the ultimate and the highest goal to which man can aspire…I understood how a man who has nothing left in this world may still know bliss, be it only for a brief moment, in the contemplation of his beloved."

I've read many accounts of people in extreme life-or-death circumstances, and always, when a person thinks it's all over, the one thought they have is of the person they are closest to, whether it is their spouse or child or parent or best friend. The closest bonds we have are the highest value we know.

And you can *cultivate* these close bonds. You can take steps to help them develop, or you can accidentally do things that impede their development.

You can't create a deep bond with just anyone. Some people are incompatible. But you can make mere affection deepen into a profound bond, and you can do it with the following principles:

1. Work together for a purpose. A truly meaningful bond will emanate out of a strong purpose. The two of you can share a purpose, or one of you can have a purpose the other supports and believes in. Comradeship goes beyond friendship, and a shared purpose is the main reason it does.

2. Believe in your comrade. When Stephen King was a laundry worker with a dream to be a writer, he wrote several novels that were all rejected by publishers and agents. All that work for nothing! He didn't even get personal rejections. He got form letters. It was pretty disheartening.

As he started to work on his fourth novel, demoralization set in. He'd been spending every spare cent sending manuscripts to agents and publishers. There were bills to pay and all this writing was obviously getting him nowhere. He was spending his nights and weekends typing and typing and typing, and for what?

So one night he threw away the manuscript he was working on. But his wife was a true friend. She believed in him. So the next day she pulled the manuscript from the trash and said, "You shouldn't be quitting. Not when you're so close."

He went back to punching out fifteen hundred words a day. Without much feeling of hope, he sent off the manuscript when he finished, but this time he struck gold. The manuscript was *Carrie*. It sold five million copies and was made into a hit movie.

3. Be loyal. The act of loyalty intensifies the bond. Be clear what I'm saying here. I'm not saying that when you have a very close bond, you will feel more loyal, although you very well might. I'm saying the act of loyalty *itself* makes you closer.

If you are true to someone, be *true*. Defend them in their absence. Stand by them in times of trouble. Speak well of them behind their back. Look for opportunities to act in their best interests when nobody is looking and when everybody is looking. This is loyalty, and it is a *choice*, an act of will, and that's what makes it valuable.

4. Fulfill trust. You have the option to commit your time or your resources or your effort. You can decide to commit or not. And when you commit yourself, you then have another option: whether or not to honor that commitment. A truly meaningful bond can develop when you consistently fulfill your comrade's trust in moments of temptation. You will become a better person for the discipline to do it, and your bond will grow stronger. Trust is powerful, but it can easily be destroyed. Protect that trust with all your might.

5. Speak honestly. In the introduction to Russell Gough's *Character is Destiny*, he writes, "For Aristotle, the truest friendship is far more than mere companionship, mutual hobbies, and a common network of acquaintances. Friends in the highest sense of the term are those who make a conscientious effort to take ethics and personal character seriously and inspire each other to be better — in thought, in action, in life."

An important part of feeling a satisfying closeness is the feeling that you are *known*, and if you're hiding something, you know you aren't completely known by your comrade, and that will prevent you from feeling as close as you could be.

6. Happily make sacrifices for your comrade. Before Earnest Shackleton made his legendary British expedition on the Endurance, he had tried and failed to be the first to reach the South Pole. On that earlier trek, one of his crew was Frank Wild, who became Shackleton's indispensable second-in-command on the Endurance.

On that earlier trek, the four-man crew made it to within two hundred miles of the Pole, but had to turn back. As it was, they barely made it back alive. The trip back was horrendous. They were pushed almost beyond human limits. At one point, Frank Wild was suffering from dysentery and their food supplies were dangerously low. Wild wrote this in his journal: "Shackleton privately forced upon me his own breakfast biscuit, and would have given me another tonight had I allowed him. I do not suppose that anyone else in the world can thoroughly realize how much generosity and sympathy was shown by this: I do, and by God I shall never forget it. Thousands of pounds would not have bought that one biscuit."

One of the most significant acts of friendship is sacrifice — *willing* sacrifice, the kind where you *happily* give up something. Oddly enough, this act gives a sense of meaning to life that nothing else does.

7. The fewer you have, the more powerful the bond. To really develop an extraordinary uniting force with someone, you will spend lots of time with the person. For you to get to know each other, it takes time. And if you are simultaneously trying to nurture four other friendships, you cannot bond as deeply with them. There isn't enough time in the day.

Comradeship is different from acquaintanceship. It goes further than merely entertaining each other. Comradeship is manifested in action, not just in talk. It's teaming up with someone, not just hanging out with them. It takes a lot of time, and the more comrades you have, the less depth you will have with any one of them.

A recent study at the University of Michigan's Institute for Social Research demonstrates this principle. They found that women with a smaller number of friends were more content with their lives than those with a larger group of friends. Of course. The more friends you have, the more superficial those friendships are by necessity. It's a limitation of time.

If you would like a more profound bond, concentrate on a very few or just one, and forge it into something transcendent.

THESE ARE THE SEVEN most important principles of comradeship. Your bond will give your life a profound strength and love and meaningfulness and contentment that you just can't get from any other source.

1. Work together for a purpose.
2. Believe in your comrade.
3. Be loyal.
4. Fulfill their trust.
5. Speak the truth.
6. Happily make sacrifices for your comrade.
7. Cultivate very few comrades or only one.

E-Squared

WHEN HE WAS A TEENAGER, my son and I got into an argument. He got defensive and uppity, I got intrusive and sarcastic. I ended the conversation by slamming his bedroom door behind me.

At times like that, I can feel myself wanting to keep up a wall between me and the other person. I wanted to keep making my son wrong. I wanted to see everything wrong about him.

Then I remembered E-Squared (or E^2). E^2 will increase your impact on the person you're talking to — it'll add a subtle, relaxed quality to your demeanor that will help the *other* person feel at ease in your presence.

And you'll like what it does for *you* even more. You become calm and at ease and you get a strong feeling of standing on solid ground. I call it E^2 for "experienced experience."

As each moment goes by, you and I have an ongoing stream of experience — lots of sights, thoughts, sounds, feelings, smells — but we don't register much of it consciously. And that's fine. Nothing wrong with that for the most part.

But sometimes it's pretty useful to register your experience consciously. One of those times is when you feel uncomfortable or when you're upset with someone and you think you are going to lose your cool. Another might be when you're giving a speech and you feel like running away or when you're telling someone something they don't want to hear.

At times like those, pay attention to your physical experience. *Experience* your experience. Feel all the different sensations in your body.

When you are feeling powerful emotions, there is a lot to pay attention to; emotions are complex; they move through your body producing physical sensations in many different places in your body, and they change. Pay attention to the sensations and how they change.

And while you're paying attention to your physical sensations, you'll notice certain muscles — in your back, in your face, in your shoulders — have contracted and held the contraction. You'll probably notice lots of sensation in your solar plexus region.

Pay attention to everything — your body posture, the expression on your face, the light coming into the room, the sounds around you. Notice your breathing, feel your feet on the floor. *Be there.*

Simple? Sure. Obvious? Absolutely. It is nothing more than experiencing something that you are already experiencing. What could be easier?

But sometimes we don't *want* to experience our experience, and it is times like those you have to do it consciously and deliberately. Otherwise you will tend to *act out* those negative feelings or do something in an attempt to avoid feeling those feelings — something you may regret later.

So I took a deep breath, relaxed, and for a moment I paid attention to my ongoing experience: I noticed my body posture, the expression on my face, the different sensations in my body, the feel of the air on my skin, etc.

Then I went back, a changed man, and talked to my son. Those few moments I took to E^2 altered me. They stopped me from reacting — defending and attacking — and allowed me to start fresh. I went back to his room and apologized for slamming the door and explained myself as best I could. I was completely calm and had no edge in my voice, on my face, in my body, or in my experience.

He listened. He knew he'd made a mistake but I had nailed him so hard, he didn't want to admit it before. We ended the conversation with no hard feelings.

E^2 is an act of will. It's not a thought. It's not a physical action. It's a change of heart. Instead of running, you stand and feel. Instead of wanting to hide, you open yourself up. Instead of cowering inside, you pay attention and relax.

Try it. Try it any time you feel like pulling away or shrinking back. Stand firm. Breathe deep. Relax your tensions. And *feel.*

Practice E-Squared now and then:
Pay close attention to your ongoing experience.

Early in the journey you wonder how long the journey will take and whether you will make it in this lifetime. Later you will see that where you are going is HERE and you will arrive NOW...so you stop asking.

— Ram Dass

I never want to arrive. I love the ride.

— Coco J. Ginger

How You Measure Up

YOU OFTEN COMPARE YOURSELF to others. We all do. You look at the way people look and sound and move, and you check how you measure up. When you stop at an intersection in your car, you watch people walk across the street and you pass judgment on the person's hairstyle, the way they dress, and so on, and you don't even *try* to do it. It's completely automatic.

You may not be able to stop yourself from doing it. But you can *change the way* you do it.

When you compare yourself to people, you look to see how they're *different* from you. And when you look at another and note your differences, it makes you feel superior if the comparison turns out in *your* favor and inferior if it turns out in *their* favor.

When you feel superior, your feelings are communicated subtly through the way your body moves and through your voice tone, and this can make the other person feel inferior. All this mental nonsense creates a general feeling of alienation — it affects your attitude and your relationships.

But there's another option. Instead of looking for differences, you can look for *similarities*.

Look and listen to people and notice how they are like you. Our feelings of friendliness toward people are affected by how *alike* we feel.

When you know someone is from your home town or went to your college or is the same religion, you automatically feel more kinship with them. When you look for similarities you increase your feelings of compassion and affection toward that person.

Where you once felt bad about yourself from an unfavorable comparison or made the *other* person feel bad because you found him to be inferior, there will now be good feelings.

Try it the next time you catch yourself judging a person or when someone annoys you. Open your mind to notice your similarities. Recall times when *you* acted in a similar way.

Studies show that most of us have a tendency to think the bad actions of others stem from personal motives, yet we tend to think our *own* bad actions are caused by circumstances beyond our control. This causes unnecessary bad feelings between people, which is bad for your health and bad for your relationships.

Actively looking for similarities is an antidote. It is a new habit, so it will take some practice, but the process is enjoyable and the end result is too.

Notice how other people are similar to you.

To love a man enough to help him, you have to forfeit the warm, self-righteous glow that comes from judging.

— Ron Hall

Union Break

A FRIEND TOLD ME she changed her mind about a goal of hers. It had been important to her for a long time, but she decided to change the goal. I listened and then told her what I thought, off the top of my head.

But I hadn't really thought about it, and she didn't like my response. If I'd thought about it, I would have realized it was an important decision for her — too important to make casual off-hand remarks about. But I succumbed to the normal social pressure to respond right away.

This chapter is about a simple habit that could have tremendous consequences in your life: The habit of taking a break to think before responding. The truth is, if you do not *have to* respond immediately, sometimes it's better not to.

When someone says something to you or asks you for something, ask yourself, "Do I *have to* respond right now?" If the answer is no, give yourself some time to think about it. This policy is better for everyone in the long run.

This question is an important one, because it puts you in better control of your own life. Salespeople don't like it when potential customers say, "I'll think about it." Why? Because when people think about it, they are more likely to decide against it.

Sure, when the salesperson is right there singing the praises of something, and you've got all the pros dancing in your head and none of the cons, it looks good. Plus you have the social pressure of the salesperson really wanting you to buy it. So although it's a good time to make a decision that would be good for the salesperson, it's not a good time to make a decision that's right for you. Do you have to respond immediately? No, you don't. Give yourself some time. Do what's best for you.

That's true with salespeople, and it's true with a request your child makes of you, and with an answer your friend wants you to give, and when your mother-in-law wants you to do something.

You hardly *ever* need to respond immediately. But it often *feels* like you do, doesn't it? It's social pressure. Of course it's sometimes better for the *other* person if you respond immediately, but that's not usually a very good reason to do it.

"Hi, is this John?"

"Yes. Hello."

"Hi. This is Janet. Sorry to call you so late, but I really need to ask you a favor. Tomorrow morning, I have to take an early flight and I need a ride to the airport."

"What time?"

"The plane leaves at 6:05."

John is on the spot. It seems like he has to respond immediately, and of course Janet would like him to, but he doesn't have to. Unless he knows for sure the answer is yes or no, he ought to give himself time to think.

"I'll tell you what, Janet. I need a little time to think about this. Can I call you back in a half hour?"

"Well...sure. I know it is short notice. I'm sorry about that. But, yes, think about it, and I'll be up for at least the next half hour."

"Okay. I'll call you. Talk to you soon."

"Bye."

John bought himself some time to consider what would be best for him. Is Janet a good friend, or does he *want* her to be a good friend? How inconvenient will it be for him? Does Janet reciprocate? Or does she only take and not give back? Even thinking it through on his own for five minutes, he will make a better decision than he would on the spur of the moment, especially if he knows a few key principles about thinking.

Thinking about something, as in "thinking it over," is best done by asking questions about the likely results of different actions. If you have more time and it is an important decision, you can consider more options.

If you're thinking about whether you ought to take the new promotion in another town or stay where you are, for example, you need to ask questions: Will I get another opportunity? Or is this a once in a lifetime deal? How will a new town affect my life? Is it worth losing what I have — my friends, etc.? Think about the *consequences* of each possible decision you could make.

A few weeks ago, my wife and I got into an argument. We were angry with each other. I was on my way out the door to go for a walk when it started, and I decided to go for my walk before we tried to resolve anything. When I got back, we worked it out smoothly and quickly — because we'd had time to think about it. If we had tried to resolve it at the time it happened, it would probably have been a long, painful argument like we often had when we first got married, because in the flush of anger, "working it out" only means one thing: Making the other person see how wrong they are (or how right you are).

In our twenty-nine years of marriage, the single most difficult lesson I've had to learn is to refrain from trying to resolve an argument *immediately*. For some things in life, the harder you try, the *less* likely you are to get what you are trying for. Arguments are like that. The more urgent or insistent you are, the deeper into the argument you sink, until eventually you can't get out, or even remember what started it!

When you're upset and when your heart is pounding, your mind isn't thinking at its highest level. The centers of your brain responsible for dipassionate, accurate, rational thought are overpowered by parts of your brain that only think in terms of survival: Defend, attack, run, hide. And those modes are not good for working out differences between two people in a modern, civilized society.

Your brain is running on Survival Mode. Take a break. Go in the other room. Go for a walk. The relationship will be there in an hour — if it won't, it wasn't much of a relationship to begin with.

The other person might not want you to leave. They might follow you out the door, trying to keep you talking. They might be in Survival Mode too, and feel the need to work things out immediately. Assure them it'll be a short break, and then you'll talk about it. Say to them, "I need to cool off and think about this because I'm not thinking so clearly right now."

It may take some trials and failures to remember to take a break during an argument and exert the discipline to actually do it, but this habit will make your arguments less destructive.

Of course, it's possible that when you come back after a break, the argument erupts and you stop being rational again (or the other person does). Take *another* break. Even if you have to do this for two weeks, it's better for the relationship than trying to work things out in an irrational state of mind.

You and I are animals. We have responses we might wish we didn't have. We didn't design our nervous system, and it didn't evolve to make us happy.

Let's be responsible for it. I don't mean "it's our fault so let's feel bad about it." Let's be "responsible" for it in the same way if you have bad eyesight, you take responsibility for it and wear glasses or contacts. You don't try to wish it away or pretend it's not there. It is the way it is. There is nothing you can do about it other than adapt yourself to the reality of it.

Taking a break when you feel insane is a way to adapt to the biological reality of your body.

So whether someone has given you important information, or someone is asking you for a favor, or if you're upset, remember this simple principle:

When you don't need to respond right away, take a break and think it through.

To him that waits all things reveal themselves...

— Coventry Patmore

Wise men speak because they have something to say; fools because they have to say something.

— Plato

Wise men, when in doubt whether to speak or to keep quiet, give themselves the benefit of the doubt, and remain silent.

— Napoleon Hill

Necessary Conflict

CHILDREN TRY TO TRAIN their parents as much as parents try to train their children. Children want their parents to wait on them hand and foot, to buy them whatever they want, to grant them freedom and privilege, and to think everything they do is wonderful.

If you have children, you know this is true. They want a lot from you. And they use whatever tools they can to attain it: throwing a fit, being cute, whining, wearing down resistance with persistence, lying, trying to use your own rules against you, pitting Mom against Dad, pretending to go along with you in order to gain favor, being "good," trying to make you feel guilty, etc.

You're familiar with the techniques. Every kid invents them anew and uses whichever techniques he can get away with.

I've seen parents counter their children's strategies with "That makes Mommy unhappy," as if Mom's happiness is on the child's top-priority list. I'd hate to break the news to a mom who says this, but her happiness is way down there, below cookies and new toys.

The motivation a child has to please a parent is weak compared to the motivation to gain more resources and privileges. For example, about 61 percent of parents give their children an allowance. A little more than half of them start the allowance when the kid is only eight years old. How many of these kids, do you suppose, save any of their money? Only one percent. Most of them take that money and buy toys and candy. That's what they want. Come on, you were a kid once. Did you ever recall centering your day around what would make your parents happy? Was that what occupied your mind?

These hard truths mean that if you have a child, you must arrange it so there is a strong motivation to do what you want — something more powerful than "It makes me happy."

It's not that your child doesn't care about you. It's that the self-discipline it takes to be fair and sacrifice one's own wishes for the good of someone else and for the long term is *learned*. It's not inborn. So while your child *does* want to please you, he also wants cookies and if he can get them by being nice, he will. If he can get them by screaming, he will.

Now that you're an adult, you know it's important to delay gratification. You know vegetables are better for you than cookies. And you have enough appreciation for long-term consequences that you're willing to sacrifice pleasure in the moment. But your child isn't.

So the two of you are going to conflict.

In any conflict, failure to be aware of the goals of the other person puts you at a disadvantage in gaining your own goals. You want to buy her a book. She wants more junk (toys). You want her to eat vegetables and protein. She wants cookies and ice cream. You want to teach her manners and morals. She wants you to go pester someone else.

By and large, your children are not the slightest bit interested in most of what you really want to give them.

Your goals are in conflict. That is the way it is. You cannot make your goals align without compromising your integrity, so *you* must be the one who sets the standards and *you* must deal out consequences when the standards are violated.

Reasoning won't work with someone who hasn't had enough experience to appreciate long-term consequences. So you have to create immediate consequences. And the consequences have to be more of a deterrent than the pleasure your child gets from violating the standard.

Knowing you're disappointed usually won't do it. "A good talking to" won't either.

You need something sufficiently difficult, inconvenient, or painful to make a child choose wisely: a week without dessert, no TV for three days, extra chores.

And it only works when you follow through and enforce the consequences.

This is an important conflict. The way it turns out makes a difference. It's your adult standards against your child's whims. It's conscience against genetically driven impulse. It's experience against ignorance. Who will win? For your sake and for your child's sake, I hope it's you.

Accept the natural conflict between parent and child.

Set standards and enforce them with consequences.

You can't make your kids do anything. All you can do is make them wish they had. And then, they will make you wish you hadn't made them wish they had.

— *Marshall B. Rosenberg*

We're Family

IN THE MOVIE, *MADE IN AMERICA*, a daughter raids the files at the sperm bank her mother used, and despite her shock in finding out her dad is an infamously slick car salesman, she loves him because he's her dad. Everything is beautiful until they discover it was a mistake. He really wasn't her dad after all.

She loved him because *she thought he was her dad.* Most of us are like that. We have an automatic acceptance of people in our family — even a distant cousin we meet for the first time.

What if we treated *all* people as relatives? If they are older, we could imagine them as uncles or aunts or great uncles or great aunts. If close to your own age, they could be long lost siblings or cousins. Youngsters could be your nieces and nephews.

Love comes naturally when we haven't labeled someone as "other." And it's really not much of a stretch. In truth, we all are related in one way or another, probably more closely related than you'd think.

According to the experts on genetics, you wouldn't have to go very far back in time to find where your family tree intersects with your friend's or spouse's family tree, or the family tree of anyone you know.

And as you keep going back, the trees cross again and again. We are all, at the very least, distant cousins of one another many times over.

Keep this in mind when you interact with people and the world will feel like a friendlier place.

This doesn't mean you have to become an easy target for con artists. You don't have to turn off your good judgment. But you interact with people every day: the bus driver, the clerk at the store, a neighbor, the people you work with. Think of them as family and you'll feel differently toward them, and that'll make you *act* differently toward them, which will make *them* act differently toward you, and *voilà!* The world is a friendlier, happier place for real.

Practice it on the next three people you talk to, and you'll see what it's like. In your mind, imagine the person is a relative. You don't have to *do* anything differently. Simply entertain the idea that the person may be a relative of yours.

We know intellectually we're all members of the same human family, but it's nice to *feel* it too.

When you talk to people,
think of them as relatives.

The true sign of intelligence is not knowledge
but imagination.

— *Albert Einstein*

Mastery

SOMETHING IS HAPPENING. After an entire generation of parents and teachers have worked hard to improve their children's self-esteem, the level of depression in young people has skyrocketed. And according to Martin Seligman, PhD (a researcher who has spent his lifetime studying depression and ways out of it), the two are intimately linked.

In his book, *The Optimistic Child,* Seligman writes, "By emphasizing how a child feels at the expense of what the child *does* — mastery, persistence, overcoming frustration and boredom, and meeting challenges — parents and teachers are making this generation of children more vulnerable to depression." And he's got a lot of research to back him up.

There's nothing *wrong* with trying to improve a child's self-esteem. Feeling good about yourself is healthy and valuable. But the *way* you improve self-esteem makes a big difference. When it is done with compliments, even if children feel better about themselves, they will be more vulnerable to depression when they hit one of life's inevitable setbacks. They may feel good about themselves, but if they are weak and incompetent, life will eventually give them failure and heartbreak and possibly depression.

On the other hand, if we try to improve our children's self-esteem by helping them learn to overcome barriers and to persist in the face of frustration, if we help them learn to tolerate discomfort long enough to succeed at something, we've given them real and valuable gifts.

Their confidence and belief in themselves will be based in *reality*, not merely in what people have *told* them. It's a confidence that cannot easily be shaken. It's a resilience that cannot easily be crushed.

This way of building a child's self-esteem is harder on the adult and it's harder on the child — in the short run. It's quicker and easier to just say nice things.

But in the long run, a sense of *competence* will do more for a child than any nice things you could tell them. Actions speak louder than words. The child's own actions and the responses they get from the world speak louder than any words, no matter how pretty.

Let's give our children something *real:* competence. And from that competence, they will have a self-confidence that renders them immune to depression. The gift of mastery has no equal.

Improve children's self-esteem
by helping them become more competent.

I want to distinguish between warranted and unwarranted self-esteem. And I think our hedonistic nation has become a nation that doesn't much care how you get your self-esteem and would prefer to inject it directly.

— *Martin Seligman*

Take the Sting Out

CRITICISM HURTS. So nice people like you try to avoid criticizing others. But sometimes you can't avoid it forever, so finally, when you get mad enough, you speak. The problem is, when you criticize while you're mad, you aren't likely to do it *well.* You'll say what the person did wrong instead of saying what you want him or her to do differently in the future. And when you say something while you're angry, the listener gets defensive because anger is an attacking emotion.

One way of getting around this is to speak *sooner.* Criticize *before* you get angry. Criticize when it first occurs to you and you won't have to "try to control yourself."

When you say it sooner, you will naturally and easily have more control over yourself. And people won't get very defensive because you're not attacking them. Oh, they might not like it. Not many people *like* being criticized. Most of us would prefer everyone loved us and showered us with praise for just being ourselves. But that's not the way the world is. Criticism is a necessary part of relationships of any kind.

Look at what happens to someone who *never* gets criticized. There have been dangerous people who had so much power that everyone was afraid to criticize them: Hitler. Stalin. Saddam Hussein. It made them lose touch with reality. You and I *need* criticism even though we don't like it.

And we need to criticize people. Not all the time, and it needs to be balanced with acknowledgments, but you can't go around only complimenting people — it isn't good for the people you work with or who live with you. You must criticize.

But say it *early*. Minimize the pain for both of you by not procrastinating. Say it while it is still a mild irritation. You'll say it better, the person will hear it better, you'll cause less pain and have more of an impact — the kind of impact you *want* to have on people: considerate and constructive.

And remember how to make a good criticism: Don't say what you didn't like; say what you would like in the future. Turn your complaint into a request. Which would you rather hear: "You never pick up around here" or "Would you please pick up around here more often?" In other words, don't make them wrong for what they've done; just tell them what you want next time.

Speak up sooner and when you do, make requests. The end result is you'll get more of what you want from people, and they (and you) will be happier.

Criticize earlier, but first turn your criticism into a request.

Criticism may not be agreeable, but it is necessary. It fulfills the same function as pain in the human body. It calls attention to an unhealthy state of things.

— *Winston Churchill*

Receiving Criticism

GETTING CRITICIZED used to upset me. And because it was so upsetting, I was somewhat afraid of criticism. It often stressed me out more than was necessary. I decided to change this. So I started reading.

It's amazing to me that almost every time I try to find out something, I can find it. Usually someone has written an entire book on the subject.

I found what I was looking for in a book called *Heart of the Mind*, which has a practical mental strategy for handling criticism. There's another version of the same strategy in the book, *Change Your Mind — and Keep the Change*. The strategy uses "dissociation." In neurolinguistic programming (that's what those two books are about), "dissociation" means being outside your body in your imagination. It is contrasted with being *associated*, which means looking at the world from inside your body.

To illustrate the difference and make it clear what I'm talking about, right now imagine what it would be like to get up and go to the bathroom. Stay where you are, but *imagine* you are in the bathroom, walking back to where you really are.

Can you see yourself sitting here reading this book? Can you see what you would look like *from across the room?* Can you see the position of your body? That's being dissociated. Your point of view is outside your body in your imagination.

Now remain dissociated and imagine you're still looking at yourself reading this book and someone comes up and interrupts your reading to criticize you. You're standing there watching the other person criticize you, but you are watching *from outside yourself*, seeing what the other person looks like and seeing what *you* look like from outside your body, dissociated. Can you see it wouldn't bother you as much that way? Since you feel separated from the situation, you are somewhat distanced from your feelings.

I just ran across an example of someone spontaneously using dissociation to relieve the anguish of something much more significant than criticism. Viktor Frankl said one day he was suffering very badly in one of Hitler's concentration camps. The prisoners had to march out to a remote area and it was very cold. They didn't have much clothing on and they were drastically and chronically underfed.

Frankl had thoughts going through his mind about things that were important to him at that time. If he got a little piece of sausage in his soup tonight (as sometimes happened) should he trade it for a piece of bread? Where could he get a piece of wire or string to replace the little piece he'd been using as a shoelace? And on and on.

Frankl felt disgusted that he had to think about such petty things. He was a psychiatrist before the Nazis took control. He was used to thinking about more meaningful or important topics than sausage and shoestrings. Now his mind was consumed by trifling, irritating thoughts in his daily struggle for survival. So he forced himself to think about something else, and he spontaneously dissociated. He pictured himself in front of an audience lecturing about the "psychology of the concentration camp!"

"All that oppressed me," Frankl wrote, "became objective, seen and described from the remote viewpoint of science. By this method I succeeded somehow in rising above the situation, above the sufferings of the moment, and I observed them as if they were already of the past. Both I and my troubles became the object of an interesting psychoscientific study undertaken by myself."

Dissociation is very effective for distancing yourself from emotional pain. The strategy from *Heart of the Mind* uses dissociation. I took their strategy and modified it a bit. I memorized my modified strategy, which I'll describe in a minute, and then I was ready to practice.

My wife, Klassy, helped me by telling me *real* criticisms that were gradually more and more difficult to hear while I took my time and went through the strategy one step at a time. It took us about an hour and a half. By the time I was done, even the very hard-to-hear criticisms did not bother me *at all.* I could not believe it! Here is the strategy I used:

1. Climb into the fort. First I created a safe place in my imagination. I climbed up a ladder into a solid steel fort surrounded by armed guards. It felt totally safe. In the fort I had a television monitor with no sound, and a printer. The scene on the screen was the place I was in actuality. But I didn't see the scene from my own eyes. It was from an upper corner of the room, like a surveillance camera. This allowed me to dissociate from the scene.

Let's say my boss walks up to criticize me for showing up late for work. As soon as I recognize a criticism is forthcoming, I imagine climbing up the ladder. I'm no longer in my body. I'm visually dissociated. I'm watching the scene on my video monitor. On the screen I see both my boss and myself from a vantage point out and away from the two of us, as if there was a camera across the room pointing back at us.

2. Read the printer. In the fort, I can't hear what my boss is saying. But I can read it as it is being printed. This is a further dissociation — auditory dissociation. So I use auditory *and* visual dissociation. I added this because the two things that triggered the most negative emotion in me during a criticism was the look on the person's face and the tone of their voice. Having to read the message removed the tone of voice but kept the information.

3. See if it's useful. So I'm looking at the monitor seeing my boss talking to me. I read what he's saying. Having removed myself from the immediate frontal onslaught, looking at myself from the side and reading the message, I eliminated almost all of the feelings I normally associated with that kind of communication. I had a neutral feeling — not a negative feeling, not a positive feeling. Just kind of detached and observing. Then I evaluated the criticism as information to determine whether this information was useful to me or not. And this is the beauty of the strategy. You can gain information.

A lot of criticisms, even when they are said with outright cruelty, contain information that could be useful to you. Some people, in order to avoid the pain of criticism, learn to simply reject all criticism. They aren't bothered by criticism, but they also don't get the useful information it might have contained.

This method protects you from having to feel the pain, but doesn't block you from gaining the information.

THAT'S THE STRATEGY: 1) climb into the fort and look at the video screen, 2) read the printer, and 3) see if any of it could be useful to you. This strategy might seem complex at first, and it felt a little awkward when I first did it because it was unfamiliar. But after a few times, it started to feel pretty natural. And the fact that the pain was gone was wonderful! I remember toward the end of our training session, Klassy was throwing some harsh, *genuine* criticisms at me and they didn't bother me at all. And the fact that they didn't bother me made me happy! It felt like I had been imprisoned my whole life — hemmed in by the fear I might be criticized. Suddenly the jailer was gone and the door was unlocked. I was free!

I realize now that my response to criticism before was about the *criticism*. Rather than paying attention to the actual *content* — the information in the statement — I was noticing and responding to what it all meant and how it was said and what emotions were being transmitted and whether or not I felt rejected and whether or not they felt disappointed in me. I would simply get demoralized and distressed by criticism or I would get angry or embarrassed, or whatever.

All of this is a lousy response to a criticism. It may be a "valid" way of listening to criticism, but it isn't at all helpful for either me or the other person. It feels bad to me, and the other person has the frustrating experience of not really feeling their message got through. It's as if a person was trying to tell me to get out of the middle of the street because there is a car coming and my response was to stand there feeling indignant at her tone of voice. Imagine how frustrating it would be to her because she's trying to tell me something important and I'm ignoring what she is saying and only paying attention to *how* she's saying it.

The most important question is: Is this information *useful* to me? Usually when someone is criticizing you, they are telling you something important to you. And if it isn't important to you, there is no need to have a negative feeling.

This is easy to say, but you have to know *how* to do it. You need a strategy. You can't just tell yourself, "Don't feel that way." Not very many people know how to change their feelings at will.

Your response to a criticism *could* be: "Thanks for telling me that!" I now find myself often feeling *thankful* for a criticism. But you can't really respond that way to unexpected criticism unless you are paying attention to the content of the criticism and how it relates to your goals. And you can't really do that unless you are dissociated.

Not many people know about this idea, and that's a shame. You could truly make the world a better place by teaching others how to do this. People are sensitive to criticism because it's so painful. And it's so painful because we take it like a bazooka blast to the chest.

But that's just *one* way to take it. There are other ways, and just about any of them work better than the one we usually use.

Some ways make criticism painful and cause hard feelings between people who love each other, and some ways allow people to receive criticism without pain. You now have a choice.

When receiving criticism, dissociate and look for useful information.

I take compliments and I take constructive criticism. Not everyone loves you. It's the way you react as a footballer. I use it all to make me play better.

— Timothy F. Cahill

Purposeful Relationships

IN TIMES PAST, and even now in some parts of the world, each member of a family had their fate tied up with the other members of the family. They all had to pull together or the survival of everyone was in danger. They shared a purpose. They all shared a very concrete, serious purpose that could not be ignored: Survival. And they shared the purpose with each other but not with "outsiders" because the family was husband, wife and kids, and maybe also parents of the husband or wife. Sometimes siblings and cousins. They all lived together and relied on each other and so shared the same fate.

There were things to do. Urgent, *necessary* things. And of course, while human beings are accomplishing necessary things, they will also talk to each other and form relationships.

This historical reality is largely where we get our reverence for "family." It is a remnant from when conditions were different, although, of course, many families still have shared purposes.

You'll sometimes see two men who fought together in a military conflict forty years ago — men who may live in different states — and yet they still treat each other like best friends. For a short time they shared a real purpose, and that experience is so rare in this modern world, their bond shines like a beacon through the years, brighter and clearer than all the comparatively superficial relationships those men have had in the last forty years.

Purpose is essential. It is the core of a relationship. Without it, the bond is missing something important and fundamental. There may be superficial chitchat, there may be social interaction, there may be mutual entertainment. But that is nowhere near a relationship based on, centered around, and springing from a *shared purpose*. It's not even in the same league.

Times have changed. Most families don't have to pull together to survive. In fact, most families couldn't think of a unifying purpose if they had to. I don't mean "carrying on the family name." That's not a real purpose. A purpose is something you have to *strive* for. It isn't something that happens as a matter of course. These days, the purposes of the individual members of families are all diverse and unrelated. Their purposes are *unrelated*.

There are no necessities that bind us with our blood relations. No urgent, concrete things that need to be done in concert with our family members. That's what relationships are made of at the root, and so, strangely enough, many of us don't really *have* relationships with our relatives. We go through the *motions* of relating, but it's empty. We can tell there's something missing, but can't quite put our finger on it.

During the Great Depression, many families were put into a serious survival situation, and they bonded closely. Their fates were tied together. And many people who lived through it said their family had never been closer.

When a group of people put out effort for the day and it all adds together to make mutual survival during difficult times, you can eat dinner together and socialize and there will be relationships, because there is an important reason to work out your differences. But when you just eat together without the tied-together purpose, an important motivation for connection is missing.

Nowadays, people sometimes feel closer to people they work with than they do with some of their own family members. They share a purpose with their work-mates. If a married couple isn't working together to accomplish a shared goal they both feel is vitally important, they feel that something isn't quite right, but they don't know what. They might have a nice house, enjoy skiing together, and really like each other, but something is wrong. And "working on the relationship" won't do it either. The relationship itself — its health, its well-being — cannot be the shared purpose, because its health and well-being depend on a purpose outside the relationship.

This all sounds a bit harsh, doesn't it? What can we do about it? If you want to feel close to someone, family member or not, you have to find a common, serious, and important purpose and make it the central focus of your relationship.

If you find yourself not feeling close to someone and you don't know why, this is one good place to look. And if you don't have at least one important purpose you share, come up with one. If it's an important enough purpose, and if you are both committed to it, you will feel a bond that's hard to match.

Make your relationship center around a shared purpose.

How to Have More Life in Your Time

TELEVISION IS A GREAT DEVICE for creating a little diversion when we want to give our minds a break. It's one of the few things we can do that presents very little challenge. Surfing the internet is another one. The problem with both of them is that the people who design the content and the advertising don't want you to just enjoy a little break and get back to real life. They want you to keep sitting there in front of your screen. And over the years, they've developed hundreds of effective techniques to pull us in and keep us hooked, and they're getting better at it all the time.

Studies at the University of Chicago found that when people are engaged in an activity like reading a book, talking with a friend or pursuing a hobby, they become happier. I'm sure you've discovered the truth of this already. There is something peaceful, human, and satisfying about these low-tech undertakings. They make people happy. That's different than the feeling of compulsion or addiction, which is what it often feels like to watch television or surf the internet.

Research also shows that the longer a person sits in front of a screen, the more irritable and dissatisfied they become. Checking Facebook and watching television are entertaining, but they present no challenge and no face-to-face interaction with people. Our minds and bodies start going stir crazy without these things. That's bad enough, but on top of that, the advertising is specifically designed to make you feel dissatisfied (so you'll buy the product to satisfy your "need").

You've got better things to do. If you want to gain more freedom from your screens, try one of these ideas:

1. For one month, whenever you would normally watch television, watch a *movie* instead, or watch something without any commercials.

2. Cancel your cable: You'll save money and you'll have fewer stations to entice you.

3. Set some kind of limit on screen time. For the next week, for example, "I will check Facebook no more than once a day." Or "I'll get online no more than a half hour a day."

4. Unplug your television for a week.

You may thrash around like an addict in withdrawal, but hold firm and you will experience something wonderful: more good conversations, more walks at sunset, more pursuits of passions, more reading of books. More *life*. More happiness. There aren't many things as easy and undemanding as television and online surfing, but there are an almost infinite number of things more satisfying and rejuvenating.

You may feel somewhat addicted to the screen. That doesn't mean something is wrong with you. The people designing the web sites and social media and television programs have *made* it that way. They hire psychologists to who study human behavior and conduct experiments to discover what will compel your attention the most.

But you have the power to *choose* how you spend your time, how you live your life. And when you take deliberate breaks — even for a day — from one of these compelling distractions, it helps give you an emotional distance from it, making you more capable of resisting its enticements.

Wean yourself away from your television and internet surfing. Make these merely *peripheral* activities — *not* things that consume a significant part of your waking hours. You don't have to make a big change to make a big difference. Just make a small improvement, and it can start a positive chain reaction.

Try some of the ideas above to protect yourself from the deliberately addictive nature of the screen. You'll be glad you did.

Wean yourself away from watching television or surfing the internet by taking a break from it.

When you're young, you look at television and think, there's a conspiracy. The networks have conspired to dumb us down. But when you get a little older, you realize that's not true. The networks are in business to give people exactly what they want.

— Steve Jobs

Elicit Your Own Acknowledgment

EVERYONE NEEDS ACKNOWLEDGMENT. Not that we'll die without it, but it really makes a difference when we know other people know how good a job we're doing.

But not one in ten of us gets enough appreciation. A common reaction to this fact is that bosses and spouses should pay more attention; they should notice and then appreciate us.

The problem is, it is hard to notice the absence of a negative condition. When you don't create problems and do your work well, and you allow other people to do their jobs unhindered, what is there to notice? Your good job becomes business as usual.

The juxtaposition of those two facts — everyone needs acknowledgment and it is hard to notice the absence of a negative condition — presents us with but one solution: You should *elicit your own acknowledgment.* Point out your efforts to others when they don't notice.

But you can't do that! It's called bragging. And we've all met obnoxious, self-centered, boorish people who had a habit of talking about themselves and what they have accomplished. Bragging is offensive. Isn't it?

Yes it is — when it is done by obnoxious, self-centered people. When it is done by someone who simply wants to do a good job and stay motivated, eliciting acknowledgment can be a very positive thing for everyone involved.

It might go something like this: You've been particularly careful about doing a certain thing, and you've been doing it consistently. You know what you're doing really helps out. You know things are working a lot better because you're putting in the time and effort to do this thing well.

But since it helps everything go well, and since it is so difficult to notice the absence of a negative condition, no one seems to notice you're doing such a good job.

So when your spouse or boss is nearby, say to them, "I've been working very hard to make sure this thing goes right, and it's been going right. I just wanted someone to know."

Since we are all in the same boat, the person you are talking to will understand the feeling of simply wanting someone else to know, and you might even open up the possibility for him or her to do the same thing (elicit acknowledgment).

You don't have to *force* anything. You don't have to brag and swagger and say it over and over all the time until you brighten up the room every time you leave. You don't need to come from *deficiency*. You aren't *desperate* for attention. You're just helping yourself feel a little better about your work (and motivating yourself to keep it up) by letting someone know what you're doing.

Don't expect a lot. Some people will think it's strange that you pointed out your own good work. Some people will think you're bragging. Keep paying attention to the kinds of responses you get and keep modifying what you are doing until it is a simple acknowledgment of the facts.

Also, get people to talk about what *they* are doing that they want someone to know about, and then give them some acknowledgment for it. They will not only become more willing to acknowledge you for your accomplishments, but they will also be less likely to feel jealous when you point out something *you* did.

Elicit your own acknowledgment. It's way better than grumbling that no one notices. It's not anyone's fault that no one notices. Because of the way our bodies, brains and the universe is constructed, it is just that way. Not much we can do about it but *use* it. You can bemoan the fact that gravity keeps you pinned to the Earth or you can accept it and get so good at dealing with it you can dance!

When you want acknowledgment for something, tell someone what you did.

We value virtue but do not discuss it. The honest bookkeeper, the faithful wife, the earnest scholar get little of our attention compared to the embezzler, the tramp, the cheat.

— John Steinbeck

You have to give yourself credit, not too much because that would be bragging.

— Frank McCourt

Make Your Own Labels

THE FOLLOWING EXPERIMENT took place in Brooklyn: Sixty-two teenagers were assembled in a room. Labels an inch and a half high were stuck at random on each person's forehead. The labels were all different, saying things like: "Lazy," "Ugly," "Famous," "Rich," "Cool," "Clumsy," "Wimpy," etc. Each person could see everyone else's label but not his or her own, and it was against the rules to tell someone what their label said.

They were told to treat each other according to the label on their foreheads. Then they mingled.

At the end of the experiment, one young man said, "I feel distrusted, like I'm some kind of thief. I don't like it." The label on his forehead read, "Dishonest." As you might expect, the people wearing the labels saying "Rich" and "Famous" enjoyed the way people treated them.

The participants could tell, just by the way people treated them, what their label said — maybe not the exact words, but the general idea was pretty clear to each of them.

This illustrates something very useful.

For years self-help authors have implored their readers to change *the way they appear* to others: Dress well, speak with confidence, move with assurance, and smile. In other words, act like a well-liked, successful person, even if you don't feel like one at the moment.

Believe it or not, this is practical advice. All these ways of expressing yourself *are like signs on your forehead.* They tell each person you meet, just as surely as if you had it written in big letters, how she or he should treat you. These ways of expressing yourself are like signs that say, "I'm successful, well-liked, I take care of myself, and I expect to be treated with respect."

No matter what you do or how you act, you are telling people how they should treat you, and you're conveying that message whether you are trying or not.

If the sign on your forehead is already a good one, leave it alone. But if you're not getting the response from people you want, make a new label.

Act like a person who is well-liked and worthy of respect, even when you don't feel that way at the moment.

I cannot conceive of a greater loss than the loss of one's self-respect.

— Mahatma Gandhi

I'm not concerned with your liking or disliking me... All I ask is that you respect me as a human being.

— Jackie Robinson

Wish People Well

WE NOW HAVE SCIENTIFIC EVIDENCE that prayer may actually work. Researchers in California started out with about 400 patients recovering from heart problems. Half the patients received prayers (from a distance), the other half didn't. Nobody in either group was told there was any praying going on.

According to Dr. Dale Matthews, a professor at Georgetown Medical School, those patients who were the targets of prayer had half as many complications and they had *a lower rate of congestive heart failure* than the patients who were not prayed for.

Could it be? Other experiments show the same thing. In 1988, Randolf Byrd, MD, a cardiologist from the University of California at San Francisco School of Medicine started with 393 patients who had either heart attacks or severe chest pains, or both.

Half were prayed for at a distance, half weren't prayed for at all. Seventeen of those not prayed for (NPF) needed antibiotics, compared to three in the prayed-for (PF) group. Fifteen NPFs needed diuretics, compared with five PFs. Twenty NPFs had congestive heart failure; only eight PFs had it. Fourteen NPFs had cardiopulmonary arrest, compared to three PFs. Thirteen NPFs got pneumonia, compared to three PFs. Twelve NPFs needed mechanical respirators. None of the PFs did.

I'm scientifically oriented and skeptical. I think the scientific method is the best thing going to sift facts from wishful thinking. And here we have scientific evidence.

But maybe the studies are flawed or biased in some way. You can find something wrong with just about any study.

But what the heck — it might be true! So go ahead and send blessings to your friends. It can't do any harm. Send them a wish for wellness or happiness or good luck or even a specific good event like meeting and falling in love with Mr. or Ms. Right.

Whether your particular prayer has a direct effect on your friend or not, it will definitely have an effect on *you*. It feels good to send a blessing to someone even with only a vague hope it may help them.

Do what you can for the people you love. And when your day is done, it couldn't hurt — and might help — to send them good wishes too.

Send good wishes to people anytime, anywhere.

I know that when I pray, something wonderful happens. Not just to the person or persons for whom I'm praying, but also something wonderful happens to me.

— *Maya Angelou*

What to Do With a Complaint

YOU'VE HEARD PEOPLE COMPLAIN. Everybody does it at least some of the time, and many people do it a lot. A person who is complaining usually thinks he is perfectly justified because everybody knows how healthy it is to express one's anger (or annoyance or disgruntlement). It is called "venting." It is a very common and widespread belief that venting is healthy.

But psychological research has shown that the expression of the emotion of anger actually makes people *angrier*. The idea that somehow people store up anger in their bodies that then needs to be released is an inaccurate belief. It is a "common sense" idea based on a Freudian theory and seemingly backed up by the everyday observation that some things *do* seem to get rid of anger: Exercise and airing grievances. And it's true. Airing a grievance makes anger disappear. But complaining does not.

"But," you might be saying, "isn't airing a grievance and complaining the same thing?" The answer is that they are *almost* the same thing. The only difference is *who you're talking to.*

If you have a grievance with George and you tell it to *me*, you are complaining and it won't help to dissipate your anger. In fact, it has a very good chance of making your anger *worse.* But if you tell your grievance to George, your anger or feelings of annoyance are likely to vanish.

If the person who is "venting" really wants to feel better, he needs to communicate with a person who can do something about his complaint.

Therefore, I heartily recommend that you instigate this as your personal policy: All complaints should go to the person who can do something about it.

That means when someone is complaining to you about someone else, you can kindly direct them to the person who can do something about it.

This may seem a rather rough thing to do, and you can surely be as courteous and friendly about it as you are able, but it is the most sane and productive way to deal with those complaints.

And if *you* have a complaint, turn it into a request and then talk to the person who can satisfy that request.

All complaints should go to the person
who can do something about it.

Write that statement on a card and hang it on the wall. Post it at work. Memorize it. Print it on business cards to hand to people who complain to you. Perhaps I'm getting carried away.

But I'll tell you why that statement makes a good personal policy. If you have to listen to Alice complaining about Sam, you will feel social pressure to side with Alice against Sam, sympathizing with her. This will weaken your relationship with Sam (or make you two-faced). Another option you have is to defend Sam, thereby perhaps straining your relationship with Alice.

A third alternative is to say, "I think Sam is the one you ought to be talking to about this."

People will naturally complain to someone who isn't involved because it's easier than complaining to someone who can do something about it. But it doesn't improve anything.

If the complaint isn't important enough to take it to someone who can do something about it, then it isn't important enough to bother you with, either.

If it *is* important, it should probably be said — to the person who can do something about it.

This simple policy can take a negative, unproductive expression and turn it into a force for positive change.

Direct all complaints to the person who can do something about it.

True intuitive expertise is learned from prolonged experience with good feedback on mistakes.

— Daniel Kahneman

Feedback is the breakfast of champions.

— Ken Blanchard

Is That Clear?

"I TOLD HIM I NEEDED some of his staff to cover things so we could have our meeting," Ann said, "but did he volunteer anyone? No. And then today at the meeting, the supervisor asked him when he was going to have his meeting and he had the gall to say, 'As soon as Ann loans me the staff to cover it.' I don't get it!"

She doesn't get it. A lot of people don't get it. That's why I will urge you — for the sake of your sanity and effectiveness — to be overly clear when you talk to people because they tend to assume they understand when they don't. It is in your best interest to be too thorough when communicating to people. It makes you more effective.

"Don't use the one on the right," you say. "It's being repaired. Only use the one on the left."

"Sure. No problem."

Later...

"That machine didn't work," he tells you.

"Which one did you use?" you ask.

"The one on the right."

"I told you to use the one on the left!"

"No you didn't. Remember? You said I should only use the one on the right. That's what you said, I swear!"

People sometimes aren't listening very well. Sometimes they have other things on their minds. Sometimes they think they know what you're going to say already, so they don't really listen. And then there is the memory factor; human memory is certainly not the most reliable thing in the world.

You can save yourself a lot of trouble by simply repeating yourself and then questioning people to make sure they know what you said.

Be overly clear with your communication and you will experience less resentment and you'll have fewer problems to deal with later.

How can you be overly clear? By using two simple techniques: 1) repeat yourself, and 2) ask questions to make sure people understand exactly what you're saying. Be clearer than you think is necessary and you will experience less stress and more success.

Be overly clear with people.

Any problem, big or small, within a family,
always seems to start with bad communication.
Someone isn't listening.

— *Emma Thompson*

The single biggest problem in communication
is the illusion that it has taken place.

— *George Bernard Shaw*

How to Get What You Want From People

PEOPLE LOVE TO BE APPRECIATED and they hate being told they're wrong. Given that, a good way to get what you want from others is to:

1. appreciate what you like
2. ignore what you don't like
3. never indicate — even in your tone of voice or body language — you think they're wrong

Let's look at the first part: Appreciate what you like. *Strongly* appreciate anything the person does that's *in the direction* of what you want. Tell her or him why you appreciate it, how much you enjoy it, how it makes you feel, and how, specifically, it makes your life easier, happier, or whatever. Detail works better than vagueness or generalities.

It works to let people know what you want from them if you can tell them without making them feel wrong. But once they know what you want, find every opportunity you possibly can — when they do what you want — to praise it! If you want him to pick up his clothes, and he picks up one sock, praise it! Forget the stuff he didn't pick up. Keep at this and you'll see more and more of what you want and less and less of what you don't want. Be specific: What exactly do you appreciate? Why specifically do you appreciate it? Don't expect quick results. Just be consistent and *enthusiastic* with your appreciation and avoid any attempt to make him feel wrong, and you'll see a gradual shift over to what you want.

When you do this, at first you may feel somewhat awkward or uncomfortable. Most of us aren't accustomed to giving sincere, heartfelt appreciation face to face. Keep at it. Push through it. You'll find the awkwardness fades and you'll also find the rewards well worth your trouble.

Now about the second and third parts (they go together): Ignore what you don't like, and avoid making people feel wrong. If you make someone feel wrong, what will he do? Answer: Try to be right! He will make an excuse for it, he will try to justify it. He will want to make himself feel right, not change his ways. If you give someone the opportunity to feel appreciated for what he does that you like, and if you also leave the rest alone, he is very likely to change his ways. But if you make him wrong, you can actually make it *harder* for him to change.

The best way to get people to do what you want is to pretty much overlook what you don't want and enthusiastically appreciate what you do want. It's magic.

Downplay or overlook what you don't want and enthusiastically appreciate what you do want.

I will speak ill of no man, and speak all the good I know of everybody.

— Benjamin Franklin

This Too Shall Pass

A LOT OF THINGS MIGHT HELP you in your important relationships, but when you try to sift out the things that will help you the *most*, your ability to deal with conflict will be at or near the top of the list.

Would you like to experience less conflict? Would you like to feel calmer during conflicts? Would you like to resolve them easier? Here's how: Remember whatever is happening is *temporary*. There are several reasons this principle is so important.

When someone assumes her problem is permanent, it can lead to depression, according to Martin Seligman, one of the top cognitive science researchers.

Assuming something bad is permanent is one of the biggest contributors to the downward spiral of depression, and depression is the most common psychological problem people experience — and one of the most destructive.

Merely being disheartened is a mild form of depression. Although it's milder, it happens more often. When you feel disheartened, you want to stop trying. So feeling discouraged not only feels bad, it makes you less capable of dealing well with problems.

Coming from an entirely different angle, Siddhartha Buddha tried to find out what caused human suffering. By his own assessment, one of his most important discoveries was this: Because human beings fail to accept the temporary nature of things, they suffer more than they need to.

According to Buddha (and I happen to agree with him on this), this lack of acceptance that things are temporary and always changing is one of the main sources of suffering for humanity.

When Abraham Lincoln was in the White House, he experienced stress, and that is an understatement if I've ever made one! Soldiers were getting slaughtered by the tens of thousands and Lincoln was the one sending them to their tragic deaths.

He was a deeply empathetic man, so this tremendous slaughter caused him immense despair and sadness and pain. But it needed to be done, and decisions needed to be made every day.

To keep himself calm enough to deal with it, he often said to himself, "this too shall pass." He used this phrase as a kind of mantra. He was able to maintain his rationality and carry out his duties at a crucial time in history — largely by reminding himself again and again that whatever is happening is temporary.

This too shall pass. The one constant in this universe is that everything changes. Remind yourself of this and you'll suffer less. You'll get disheartened less often and less intensely. And — back to our original purpose — you'll deal with conflict better.

Try saying that phrase to yourself next time you feel upset about something. Use it as a mantra. The circumstances that caused the upset will change — maybe not all of them, but some parts of your circumstances will change all by themselves.

And remind yourself that your feelings will change inevitably, even if you do *nothing* to change them. You won't stay upset forever. I know this is obvious to you now, but when you're upset, you tend to forget this important truth.

It is, of course, a simple idea, but it can significantly ease the strain of the moment, making you better able to deal with whatever is happening to you, creating less stress in your body and mind, and making you a calmer person.

Say to yourself in times of stress:
This too shall pass.

It is said an Eastern monarch once charged
his wise men to invent him a sentence
to be ever in view, and which should be
true and appropriate in all times and situations.
They presented him the words: "And this, too,
shall pass away." How much it expresses!
How chastening in the hour of pride! How
consoling in the depths of affliction!"

— *Abraham Lincoln*

So comes snow after fire, and even dragons
have their endings.

— *J.R.R. Tolkien*

Self-Confidence

THE OPPOSITE OF SELF-CONFIDENCE is self-consciousness. To achieve self-confidence, then, all you need to do is get rid of your self-consciousness. But how? How do we get our attention off ourselves?

Easy — by putting it somewhere else. And the easiest way to have your attention on something else is to have a purpose of some kind.

Let's see how this works. Let's say you're at a party and you're feeling self-conscious. The first question to ask is "Do you have some purpose for being at the party in the first place?"

If you don't, a quick and easy way to stop feeling self-conscious would be to leave the party. But let's say you *do* have a purpose for being there.

Ask yourself, "What's my purpose here?" In other words, what do you want? What are you trying to accomplish? What are you after? Take a few moments and think about it. Would you like to make business contacts? Do you want to entertain people? Do you need information from somebody? Do you want to help bring people together? Do you want to meet someone?

The question is: What is your aim or intention? If you don't have any purpose for being there, either go somewhere where you do have a purpose or *make up* some purpose. For example, during the course of the evening your purpose could be to find someone who knows a trustworthy car mechanic.

In a place I used to work, we had stretches of time with nothing to do, yet we had to be there. It left me with no purpose. So I made up purposes or made the situation serve other purposes of mine.

Some of the employees spoke more Spanish than English, and I wanted to learn Spanish, so during the slow times, I'd teach them English and they'd teach me Spanish.

Other times I needed new ideas for a project I was working on at home, and I asked my co-workers to help me, which they were glad to do.

Accomplish a goal. Make up a goal if you have to. Do you want to get rid of your self-consciousness? Put your attention on an aim. To have self-confidence, *have a purpose.* It's that simple.

Relieve self-consciousness by focusing on a purpose.

Life is not easy for any of us. But what of that? We must have perseverance and above all confidence in ourselves. We must believe that we are gifted for something and that this thing must be attained.

— Marie Curie

Self-confidence is the first requisite to great undertakings.

— Samuel Johnson

The Power of a Poker Face

RONALD RIGGIO, PHD, had been doing research at the California State University at Fullerton for over seventeen years. He wanted to find out what makes a person attractive. He studied *charisma.*

One important factor Riggio discovered is the importance of "emotional expressivity" — the ability to show your emotions on your face so people can easily read how you feel. People who don't show much emotion on their faces don't attract us very much. That's one of his findings that seems pretty obvious.

But Riggio found something that's not so obvious: Charisma also requires the ability to *not* show some emotions at times. He calls it "emotional control." It's what I'm calling a "poker face" because when you play poker and you get an exceptionally good hand, you don't want anyone else to know. Likewise, if you get a poor hand, you don't want them to know — it gives your opponents an advantage in betting against you.

While you're playing poker, the basic rule of thumb is to not ever register your feelings overtly. The main thing that might give you away is the look on your face, so you have to show as little emotion on your face as you can.

Improving your ability to have a poker face when you need it (and *only* when you need it) can increase your effectiveness with people. Why? Because emotions are contagious when they can be seen.

When you see someone laughing, it tends to make you feel like laughing, doesn't it? Sure. And when you see someone crying, it can make you feel sad. Naturally. That's why good actors are so highly valued. They can make us feel emotions. We all have a tendency to experience the emotion we see on someone's face.

But, you may ask, what's wrong with that?

Nothing really, except sometimes. The problem is that there are some emotions you wouldn't want another to have.

Two prime examples are anger and social awkwardness. When you're angry and you show it, the other person will probably become angry or defensive or afraid to some degree — they can see on your face your blood pressure is up, and their body will respond by increasing their own blood pressure. This rising intensity tends to interfere with communication.

Something similar happens when a person feels socially awkward. When you talk with someone who feels awkward because they don't quite know what to do and it shows, *you* feel somewhat awkward, too, don't you?

Or how about when someone giving a speech feels uncomfortable up there in front of the group? Don't you also squirm in your seat a little just watching?

In these kinds of circumstances, the people would be better off and the people they're talking to would be better off if they would learn to *conceal* those particular emotions when they feel them.

We have all learned there are times when it is not appropriate to *say* certain things. You don't say to a widow at the funeral "the dude owed me money."

At certain times and for certain situations, we all know "some things are better left unsaid." Well, the emotion on your face is nonverbal, but it is still communication, and sometimes it is counterproductive to say nonverbally "I'm angry" or "I feel awkward."

The good news is that you can learn to put on a poker face when you need it. I'm not suggesting phoniness or pretending you're happy when you're angry. But there are times it helps to show no emotion on your face. It's a skill like any other, and it can be improved with practice.

Practice having a "poker face" when you feel negative emotions.

If you're playing a poker game and you look around the table and can't tell who the sucker is, it's you.

— Paul Newman

I consider social skills a bit like learning a language. I've been practicing it for so long over so many years I've almost lost my accent.

— Daniel Tammet

Everyday Creativity

YALE PSYCHOLOGIST Alan E. Kazdin did an experiment with kids who were diagnosed with "conduct disorder" — young people prone to violence, vandalism, truancy, and hostility.

Many things have been tried over the years but not much has been successful. How do you change a problem child into a *healthy*, happy, productive youngster? Theories abound; results are rare.

Kazdin tried something out of the ordinary. He taught the troublemaking kids and their parents how to think up options for handling specific kinds of situations (responses other than hostility or whatever their usual response was), and to come up with different ways of interpreting different situations.

The kids and their parents learned how to think up new behaviors and thoughts. Kazdin basically taught them how to be creative rather than always responding the same way. The result: Troublemaking was significantly reduced.

When the only response you have is hostility, that's what you do, regardless of whether it gets you the results you're after. Kazdin essentially trained these people to ask themselves, "What else?"

The parents and their kids learned to say to themselves before they responded to something, "Okay, I *could* do that (what I've always done or whatever impulse first occurs to me), but *what else* could I do?" He taught them to think of new options they hadn't thought of before.

And also he taught them to ask, "What else could it *mean?*" When someone bumped into them in the hall at school, for example, instead of immediately interpreting the bump as a hostile attack or a threat, they learned to ask themselves, "Okay, it *might* mean that, but what *else* could it mean?"

This seems like a simple solution to a difficult problem, doesn't it? But it's harder than it seems. Our brains naturally streamline our mental processes over time, making our thoughts and decisions faster and easier.

Asking yourself "What else?" makes the decision-making process more complex and *slower*. So it takes some deliberate effort to turn your mind to the task of coming up with alternative ideas. It's certainly not impossible, as Kazdin has shown, but it does take a little discipline.

This method is useful in many different ways. As I'm sitting here writing this, it's really cold outside, and even though a little while ago I had the heater turned up and I'm wearing thick, warm socks, my feet were still as cold as ice. Turning the heater up and covering my feet were obvious solutions. I did them without thinking. But they did not solve the problem. They did not get me the result I wanted (warm feet).

So I asked myself, "What *else* might work?" What else could I do?

When you ask yourself a question, it awakens a part of your brain that answers questions. Ask a question and your mind searches through all the things you've heard or know, and it often comes up with something.

After I asked the question, I remembered my wife once telling me, "If your hands are cold, cover your head." She used to live at Lake Tahoe (high in the mountains of Northern California), and she learned a thing or two about dealing with cold weather. I grew up in Southern California and didn't know much about it.

So a little while ago I put a on wool hat. My feet aren't cold any more.

What else? It's such a valuable question. It's especially useful when you've been doing something a certain way for a long time.

I'm always surprised when someone comes up with a new way to do something, because it makes me think, "Why didn't I think of that?" Once you see the new way, it seems kind of obvious. But it took *somebody* asking "What else?" to come up with it.

A couple of days ago I saw measuring spoons, but rather than having a separate spoon for teaspoons and tablespoons and halves and fourths, it was a single spoon with one end of the cupped part capable of sliding back and fourth, making the spoon bigger or smaller, and there were lines on it for teaspoon and half teaspoon, etc. Why didn't I think of that? Because I didn't ask, "What else could measure teaspoons besides the measuring spoon I'm so familiar with?"

"What else?" is an especially practical question when what you *usually* do doesn't work very well. Besides getting miffed when a certain person makes certain kinds of remarks, what *else* could you do?

You can do the dishes grudgingly, but how *else* could you do them? What other ways could you go about it? In what other ways could you *think* about it?

When you interact with your sibling, and you both end up angry, ask yourself, "What else could I do?" What *other* approaches or responses can you think up besides what you naturally or normally do?

As neurolinguistic programmers are fond of saying: "If what you're doing isn't working, *do something else.*"

Of course, you wouldn't want to try something *just* because it is different because the new idea might, in fact, be worse.

Creativity is the process of thinking up new ideas and then *rejecting* most of them. It's a two-step process. The first step is generating ideas; the second is *judging* those ideas.

Those are two different processes, and the parts of your brain involved in each process are different, so they can't really be done at the same time.

In other words, when you're thinking up alternatives, don't judge the ideas for their merits at the same time. Let your mind go. Let it come up with crazy ideas, off the wall angles, and impossible notions. This stretches your mind beyond the limits within which your thinking has been confined. Out of that loosened-up state of mind, a truly original idea and sometimes a perfect solution can suddenly become obvious. You just couldn't see it before because you were unknowingly confining your thinking about that subject within certain parameters.

Think up ideas, and keep thinking them up until you get a good one. And if it's important enough and you have the time, keep thinking up more ideas — keep asking *What else?* and see if you can come up with an even better one.

The best way to characterize "thinking" is as a dialogue. Consider thinking as a dialogue with yourself. I know that if it's with yourself it's supposed to be called a monologue, but thinking isn't done very well as a monologue because there is nothing to provoke the thoughts further. A monologue is an expression of a single line of thought. Dialogue can generate more creativity.

Have a thought and then criticize it and you have a dialogue. Ask a question and then try to answer it and you have a dialogue. Come up with an idea and then ask,

"What else?" and you have dialogue, and that's where good thinking happens.

"Well, my in-laws are coming over," says Pete to himself, "and they always drive me nuts. Maybe I'll just not say anything."

If Pete stops there, his monologue has created one idea. But this time he has a *dialogue* with himself, and thereby becomes more creative. "Yes, I could try that," he says to himself, "but what *else* might work?"

Then something occurs to Pete. "What else might work *for what?*" he wonders, "I guess I need a goal if I want to think up an idea to solve it. I need to know what I'm trying to accomplish."

"I want to feel happy even when they are here."

"Do I feel happy when I say nothing?"

"No. I've tried that before. It's not much fun. It's a little better than *being annoyed*, but I'm definitely not *happy.*"

"So what else could I do?"

"Since I want to be happy, I should do *what makes me happy*. I really enjoy playing my new video game. Maybe I can enlist one of them to play with me."

"Good idea. But I'm not going to stop there. What *else* could I do?"

"I like talking about politics. I could make that my theme for the night. I could turn every conversation to the subject of politics."

"Okay, good. What *else* could I do?"

And so on. The more Pete asks, the more he'll get. Some of his ideas will be goofy or won't work very well, but thinking is like successful photography: Take a hundred shots and you'll get a few good ones.

Creativity is like that. Generating more ideas, you have more to choose from, so your chances of getting a better one improve as the number of ideas increases. Not only that, and maybe more importantly, a new and even crazy idea can lead you into an area of thinking where you can come up with a really good and *original* idea — something out of the box, something nobody has ever thought before.

The way to get lots of ideas is to keep asking, "What else?"

Ask yourself, "What else could I do?" or "What else could it mean?" ***and keep asking.***

Creativity is a great motivator because it makes people interested in what they are doing. Creativity gives hope that there can be a worthwhile idea. Creativity gives the possibility of some sort of achievement to everyone. Creativity makes life more fun and more interesting.

— Edward de Bono

I firmly believe that all human beings have access to extraordinary energies and powers. Judging from accounts of mystical experience, heightened creativity, or exceptional performance by athletes and artists, we harbor a greater life than we know.

— Jean Houston

Creativity is the sudden cessation of stupidity.

— Edwin Land

True Love

THERE ARE BASICALLY TWO WAYS to talk to your loved ones. The first is to hide some of your true wants and feelings, either by not expressing them at all or by being so indirect and "nice" that your loved ones don't know for sure how you really feel.

The other way is to be honest about what you want and feel.

The results of these two approaches are drastically different. When you hide what you really want and feel, guess what? You *still* want and feel those things. Remember that point; it is important.

You're afraid to say what you really want and feel because you think you'll be rejected, disapproved of, or disliked. The love might be withdrawn. Saying what you want or feel might start a fight or hurt someone's feelings.

Even though you have all these perfectly valid reasons to refrain from speaking up, that doesn't alter the fact that you *still* feel what you really feel and want what you actually want.

And those wants and feelings will come out, one way or another. Consciously or unconsciously, you will try to manipulate the other person into doing what you want and your feelings *will* be expressed, no matter how hard you try to hide them.

There are many ways your true feelings might be expressed. You can hint, tease, argue about it indirectly, try to make the other person feel guilty for not doing something, "accidentally" make mistakes, and so on. Not to mention that your body language and the subtle expressions on your face give you away. Your wants and feelings come out, even against your will.

The problem with these indirect, nonverbal, and often unconscious ways of communicating your feelings and wants is that *they are confusing.* And confusion causes problems in close relationships.

It is difficult to be honest, and it can sometimes cause an upset. *But honesty is not confusing.* When you are saying what you really want and feel, problems can be worked out and solved. You can't solve a problem when you don't know what it's about.

So that's the choice: Withhold the truth or say it.

Of course, very few people are on either extreme all the time. Every one of us hides our intentions and feelings from our loved ones now and then, and at other times most of us can be pretty frank. But any effort we make to move ourselves further toward the *honest* end of the spectrum will improve the quality of our close relationships over time.

If you want to be intimate,
say what you want and feel.

We think that white lies are socially acceptable, yet we bemoan the fact that our relationships are superficial.

— M. Scott Peck

Are You Too Polite?

YOU WERE TRAINED FROM DAY ONE to be polite and attentive to the wishes of others because, of course, it is the courteous thing to do. And when you're courteous, people won't be upset with you as often and you will avoid uncomfortable confrontations and awkward moments.

It's perfectly understandable why parents would want their child to be polite. Parents do not like to be embarrassed. Besides, they want to help the child avoid being shunned by their peers. Being *rude* makes enemies. So does being selfish.

So it is important for parents to train their children to be courteous.

But there is also such a thing as "too much of a good thing." Courtesy and kindness can be *overlearned* — to the point where the person doesn't even know what he wants any more — where he'll stand there and listen to the worthless ramblings of an idiot who just likes to talk, without the guts to be "rude" and excuse himself because he's got better things to do.

Someone who has overlearned politeness will be too easily persuaded by family members that such-and-such is right and good, only to figure out later that it's not right and good for *him*, now that he thinks about it.

When you don't know what you want — when politeness dominates self-awareness — *other* people's wants hold the floor for lack of opposition. They win by default, as when two parties are scheduled for a hearing and one of the parties doesn't show. The one who shows up wins automatically by default.

What's lacking when you're too polite is a healthy level of selfishness. If you've been trained from early on to suppress your own wishes, you may suppress them right out of existence.

This kind of unhealthy politeness only happens in relation to *others*. Just about everyone can pursue their own agenda when they're by themselves. It is in the presence of other people that the social inhibitions laid down in childhood exert their powerful influence. What they influence are our feelings.

What's missing is a simple *knowledge* of what we want, what we ourselves would like to see happen, and the willingness to try to make it happen — even when someone else might not like it. And what's needed is the willingness to *say* what we want.

If you are suffering from excess courtesy, here's what to do: Start small. In little situations every day, make small goals. Ask yourself "What do I want here?" or "What do I think would be the best thing to happen in this situation?" And then try to make it happen.

Inevitably, you'll run into someone else with a different agenda. This other person has a different outcome in mind. She doesn't know about your goal. So you need to let her know what you want.

Sometimes you'll feel you're being rude. Sometimes the other person will *think* you're rude. If, like you, she's been overtrained in courtesy and undertrained in healthy selfishness, she will take up your agenda and help make it happen, or at least she won't oppose you.

If, on the other hand, she is able to say what *she* wants, the two of you can negotiate. One way or the other, you need to know what you want and you must be willing to speak up about it.

You'll be happier and more satisfied with your life in the long run if you do.

Know what you want and speak up about it.

What I must do is all that concerns me, not what the people think. This rule, equally arduous in actual and in intellectual life, may serve for the whole distinction between greatness and meanness. It is the harder because you will always find those who think they know what is your duty better than you know it. It is easy in the world to live after the world's opinion; it is easy in solitude to live after our own; but the great man is he who in the midst of the crowd keeps with perfect sweetness the independence of solitude.

— Ralph Waldo Emerson

You can't be afraid of stepping on toes if you want to go dancing.

— Lewis Freedman

Bad Apples

WHEN DALE CARNEGIE wrote his classic book on human relations, *How to Win Friends and Influence People*, he left out a chapter. It wasn't finished on time, so the book was published without it. The chapter was supposed to cover the subject of dealing with people you cannot win with.

For most people, when you treat them fairly, they treat you fairly in return. But as you know, a small percentage of people in this world will simply take advantage of you when you try to treat them fairly. There are people who will play games with you, deceive you, and some who will actively *prevent* you from making your relationship work. Carnegie's unwritten chapter was for the times when "somebody has to go to jail, be spanked, divorced, knocked down, sued in court."

Even beyond those extreme cases, every once in a while you will get stuck working with or having to interact with someone who continually brings you down or in some way makes your life difficult. They may *seem* to be very nice people. They might smile and come across with a lot of charm. But the end result of your interactions are: You're worse off. You try to make things work, you try to be fair, and you get the short end of the stick every time. You have tried to talk with them, perhaps, and it doesn't make things better, and they probably make you feel bad for saying anything.

I don't have any fancy methods for dealing with these people. You *can't* really deal with them. If they're doing something *illegal*, you can certainly call the police, but most are too clever to do something illegal. Klassy uses a good analogy in her speeches. She says trying to make things work with these people is like trying to wrestle with someone who is covered with mud: You're going to get muddy. No matter what you do or how well you do it or how noble your intentions, you'll get muddy.

So instead of trying to make things work out with these people, the goal is to avoid dealing with them at all. Go for *minimal impact*. Have as little to do with them as you can get away with (without causing *yourself* trouble). Ideally, you would eliminate them from your life completely. Stop calling, stop visiting, stop being nice. You don't have to be mean about it. Just fade them into the background and then all the way out of the picture.

I know this isn't a perfect world. Sometimes you have to keep interacting with someone who won't let you make things work. So go as far as you can to minimize their effect on your life. Talk to them as little as you can, look at them as little as you can. Focus your attention on your purpose and on the rest of the people around you.

When you come across someone and nothing works with him, cut your losses. Don't waste any more effort trying. This is a big world full of wonderful people and a few bad apples. Concentrate your attention on the good people and waste as little of your attention as you can on the ones who bring you down. You can do it a little at a time and it will improve your attitude. And if it improves your attitude, it is good for your relationships with your family and friends, and it's good for your health.

Try not to waste too much of your attention on people who bother you.

Forging Mettle

METTLE IS A WORD you don't hear much these days. It means a strength of mind that gives you the ability to withstand pain or difficulties with courage and resolve. Mettle is a quality we all admire. But it isn't something you are *born* with. It must be developed. It is strengthened by the way you conduct your everyday life. Specifically, mettle is created by daily making the decision to refuse to flinch.

You know what it means to flinch. If you pretend you are going to slug me, and I twitch or blink, I *flinched.*

Let's expand and extend that idea in a useful way: Let us say flinching is *any* form of shrinking back, pulling away or turning aside, when it's done to avoid discomfort or difficulty.

Have you ever noticed that you have a strong desire to put your hands in front of your body when you're standing up and talking to several people who are all seated? Most people do. If you *succumb* to your desire to put your hands in front of your body, that's a flinch.

Or let's say you're telling someone something she or he doesn't want to hear. While you talk, maybe you shift your body's weight from one foot to another, pick at your fingernails or cross your arms. You flinched!

If you're looking at someone and they then look at you and you quickly look away, you flinched. Mumbling or speaking quietly is a form of flinching. Someone who is avoiding going to night classes because he's afraid he might not do well is flinching.

Flinching is an attempt to protect yourself, and it's very natural. Everybody does it. But there is one major problem with it: Flinching makes you weak. Notice I did not say it was *a sign* that you are weak. The act of flinching *itself* makes you weak.

But when you have the urge to flinch and you don't, you gain a kind of strength. And when you look people in the eyes with your arms hanging by your sides where they naturally hang and you speak truthfully without flinching, you have an unnervingly powerful personal presence.

And you don't have to spend years getting good at this; you can do it the very next time you talk to someone. It's easy to do (once you decide to), but when you do it, you will notice a temptation, a craving, a desire — almost an *ache* — to fidget or look away or at least put your hands in your pockets.

Refuse to flinch.

Make up your mind — as soon as you notice yourself flinching — that you *will not* flinch. You'll like the result. A fear just goes out of you. This is especially true if you consider yourself *shy* to any degree. Don't flinch, and suddenly the sense of shyness becomes somewhat wispy and transparent, and you'll start to wonder if there has ever been anything there but a shadow.

Don't flinch, and feel the power.

Then go on and expand this power by extending the practice into the psychological arena. When a person is "in denial," it means they're mentally or emotionally flinching; they are looking away or shrinking back or avoiding something real — some truth, some reality — and always in order to avoid discomfort or difficulty.

But always and forever, wherever you flinch, you will be weak. And wherever you *refuse* to flinch, you will be strong.

This is the "how" of courage. It's not that during a courageous act a person doesn't *want* to run away. What makes it courageous is that the person wants to run away *but doesn't.* Courage is refusing to flinch.

Extend your unflinching psyche into any area where you want more personal power.

If you want to be socially strong, don't flinch in social situations. If you want to be *emotionally* strong, don't flinch at emotional feelings or situations. You could make this a lifetime practice, a spiritual regimen, a holy discipline, and it would change your life.

Wherever you refuse to flinch, you will have power. This will, of course, increase your impact on people. They will admire your courage and look up to you. When this happens, don't flinch.

Resist the temptation to flinch.

Courage is the ladder on which all the other virtues mount.

— Clare Booth Luce

If we take the generally accepted definition of bravery as a quality which knows no fear, I have never seen a brave man. All men are frightened. The more intelligent they are, the more they are frightened.

— George S. Patton

Beginner's Mind

I SEE MY WORK as beginner material. And I'm not saying that to insult my work. Not at all. The most important material in any field is *fundamental* and not elaborate or intricate or obscure or overly technical. It is beginner material. Most of the greatest gains come from the most basic principles.

For example, I know a young man who drinks wheat grass, uses healing magnets in his shoes, and drinks water only if it is filtered. But he doesn't exercise.

In my opinion, exercise is beginner material. It is basic and fundamental and would produce more real gains to his state of health and well-being than all the esoteric stuff combined.

There are thousands of studies showing how effective and important exercise is, and there are only scattered reports or mere anecdotal evidence that indicate the other three things I mentioned *might* make a small difference to your health.

There are a few things in life that are really important. All else is secondary and even superfluous. But the fundamentals are boring to inquisitive minds like ours, so our minds wander off, looking for something new and different. But to succeed and experience peace of mind you need to keep coming back to the basic fundamentals.

Earl Nightingale once had a conversation with his friend, Dr. L.D. Pankey. Nightingale was looking at a picture of one of Pankey's classes he taught for the people in his profession every year, when he noticed that there were some familiar faces — faces he'd seen in pictures of earlier classes.

"I notice many of the people who took your course a year ago took it again this year," said Nightingale, "What did you teach them this year that you didn't teach them last year?"

"Nothing," replied Pankey, "I teach them the same thing every year, not only in this country but abroad as well. Oh, I add to it each year, as I learn new things. But basically, it's the same course every year."

"Do you mean you teach the same things to the same people all over again?"

"That's right," said Pankey. He looked up at Nightingale. "When you find your golf game isn't as good as you'd like it to be," he said, "or you suddenly find the ball isn't going where you want it to go, and you can't quite put your finger on what's wrong, what do you do?"

Nightingale didn't have to think about that one. "Well, I go back to the pro for some lessons."

"That's right. And what does he teach you? Does he teach you something new about the game — something you didn't know at some time before? Or does he merely remind you once again of the basic fundamentals that, if you'll but be guided by them, will result in your getting the kind of score you'll be happier with?"

The idea of coming back to basics is *itself* a basic and needs reminding too.

And one of the most enjoyable ways to relearn the basics is to teach them to others. No doubt, as you read the chapters in this book, you will learn useful things you'll be able to teach your friends, and by teaching them, *they* will benefit and *you* will learn it better. That's a finding that has schools changing their curricula.

In tutoring programs in the past, they would take kids who excelled and let them teach kids who weren't doing very well. But recently, a different approach has shown a tremendous amount of promise: Taking average or below-average students and having *them* teach students two grades *lower* — fourth graders tutoring second graders, for example.

Studies on this approach found that the *second* graders obviously benefit, but the *fourth* graders did too. Many of them had never quite mastered some skills until they had to teach it to someone. The process of teaching the younger students allowed the older students to clarify and solidify what they had learned before. As a kind of free bonus, teaching younger students improved the attitudes of the older students and increased their self-confidence besides.

When you think you've got a pretty good grasp on something from this book, *teach it to someone.* The process of doing so will increase your own understanding, as well as giving you an even better attitude than you have now. A little more self-confidence might not be so bad either.

Helping someone else learn something fundamental will deepen your mastery of those important basics. One of the things I like most about the business I'm in — writing — is how much better I understand what I learn just by trying to explain it to you.

Stick to the basics: Your health, your relationships, your work, your peace of mind. Everything else is icing. When your frame of mind is great, when your relationships are all doing well, and when you've done what you can for your health and career for today, *then* worry about extras.

Don't spend time on icing when the basics are not in place.

If you already know the principles in this book and apply them, then read it to boost your conviction and motivation to keep on doing what you already know works.

If you know the material but don't *apply* it, then let this book motivate you to get to work. And if you come across something new here, that's great too.

But whatever you do in your life, keep to the basics — the simple, the practical, and the effective.

Stick to the few fundamentals.

You have to monitor your fundamentals constantly because the only thing that changes will be your attention to them. The fundamentals will never change.

— *Michael Jordan*

Success is neither magical nor mysterious. Success is the natural consequence of consistently applying the basic fundamentals.

— *Jim Rohn*

What Method?

WHENEVER YOU FEEL anxious, angry, upset, tense, frustrated, irritated, etc., ask yourself, "What method could I use here?"

At first you may need to browse through this book looking at the different methods. After you're more familiar with them you'll be able to do it in your head. But by making a regular practice of *applying* these principles, you'll eventually become familiar with a range of methods and asking this question will become your key tool.

Yesterday I was walking into the post office. As I stepped up to the counter, I noticed I felt more self-conscious than usual, probably because I'd had a difficult morning.

I asked myself, "What tool could I use right now?" It only took me a couple seconds to think of one. I thought, "I could use E^2."

I started doing it and *immediately* I went from feeling withdrawn to reaching *toward* the situation. It changed my state, helped me relax, and allowed me a chance to practice a good principle.

We have different tools for different circumstances. Practice one method today at work. Practice a *different* one when you're at home. Think about a result you want or a change you want to make and then rummage around in your toolbox until you find a tool that will do the job. If it doesn't work, try another one.

The all-purpose, first choice tool I use is to relax tense muscles. Walking into a tense situation, I scan my body and relax. If I am worrying about something, I relax tense muscles. If I feel just generally agitated, I relax muscles. It's my first thought, and it always helps. It's a small thing and it only helps a little, but it also takes very little time and effort.

If all you can do at the moment is take a deep breath, and it will only help a little, do it. Don't hold out for a cure-all; there may not be one. But if you can relax a little, that may be enough to make a difference.

I have a set of custom-made military dog tags with principles imprinted on them, one principle per tag. When I'm getting ready to do something, I choose the clothes I'm going to wear and I choose the principle I'm going to apply. It sounds kind of odd, but it's very practical.

What is in your mind is really far more important than which clothes you decide to wear.

Ask yourself, "What method could I use here?" You know quite a bit of useful information. You've learned a lot in your life, and you've read and heard a lot of good advice during your lifetime, but if you're like most of us, you don't apply nearly as much as you know. We're running on habits for the most part: Habits of speech, habits of action, habits of thought. It takes something out of the ordinary to wake us out of our habit-sleep and do something fresh. This question is just the thing.

Another variation on this method is asking yourself the question, "What is a good rule to follow right now?" It makes you stop and think. What are you doing or *about* to do? Is there some insight or advice you know of that, if you had it in mind right now, would make whatever you're doing go better?

Think of a good answer to that question and then *apply* that answer as you go forward. State it to yourself as a rule, and keep the rule in mind as you take action.

Many of the rules that will come to you are ones you have used before. There are three different kinds of things you can remember and use:

1. rules or principles
2. questions
3. facts

When you ask, "What's a good rule to follow right now?" good rules will pop into your head if they're appropriate. This is one of the most useful questions you can ask because you can use it in so many different situations. You know quite a bit. If you were told to write a book of truths about life, you could, and it would probably be good.

You've learned a lot during your lifetime. Haven't you ever thought, "I wish I could give *myself* advice as good as I give to other people?"

Well, here is one way to bring your accumulated wisdom out where *you* can use it. This is a way to call up your wisdom in the heat of the battle, in the midst of the fray, in the helter-skelter of an active moment.

When you suddenly feel tension, uneasiness, anger — intensely or mildly, but suddenly — that's a good time to ask this question.

Asking the question can keep you from reacting automatically. It makes you think about the situation in a way that helps you make a good response — the kind of response you'll be *glad* you made, instead of just an old habitual reaction.

Make sure those moments of sudden upset (or any negative emotion) *remind* you to ask this question of yourself. Answer it to the best of your ability and put that answer into action.

In other words, form a new habit. When you feel a negative emotion of any kind, get in the habit of asking yourself, "What method could I use here?" Or "What rule could I apply?" Concentrate on forming this habit until it is the first thing you think of every time you are upset.

One good way to make this a habit is to imagine different kinds of situations — the kind in which you would want to ask yourself the question. Imagine the situation and then ask yourself the question. Imagine another situation where you'd want to ask yourself the question. Imagine the situation and then ask the question.

Making this method a habit will, all by itself, take you to a new level of personal growth.

Ask yourself, "What method could I use here?" or "What's a good rule to follow right now?"

Anything worth doing is worth doing now.

— *Klassy Evans*

Contact the Author

I hope you enjoyed this book and will continue to enjoy it and benefit from it in the future. I would love to hear from you for any reason. Write to me at this address:

Adam Khan
c/o YouMe Works
PO Box 1703
Bellevue, WA 98009

Or email me through our web site:
www.youmeworks.com

Also on the web site, we've got bonus chapters you can read. And you can subscribe (free) to our email newsletter at www.moodraiser.com.

Other books of mine you might enjoy:

Antivirus For Your Mind
Cultivating Fire
Viewfinder
What Difference Does It Make?
Self-Reliance, Translated
Slotralogy
Fill Your Tank With Freedom
See Her Smile

ARENA

A PROFESSOR AT MESA COLLEGE in San Diego, Jim Wales, has been using this book as one of the textbooks for his class (Personal Growth 140: Life Skills & Personal Adjustment), and he has developed a process to help his students *apply* the principles (rather than merely reading and understanding them).

He calls the process ARENA, which he refers to as "a method of meta-cognition — or — learning from what you learn." He uses it as the structure in many of the Discussion Boards for the course.

If you'd like to get college credit for reading this book, you can, no matter where you live. It's an online course. In a moment I will give you his email address so you can find out more about the class if you want.

But you don't have to be in a class to use the ARENA process. Once you've decided on a principle and acted on it by putting it into practice in your life, you can use the following process — Act, Respond, Evaluate, Notice, Apply (ARENA) — to deepen its impact on your life.

1. Act — describe what occurred when you acted on the principle — when you took action. Examples of questions you can ask are:

What did you notice?
What occurred?
What was accomplished?
What happened?

2. Respond — share your reactions, discuss the importance to you. Examples of questions you can ask are:

What did you learn?
What new insights did you gain?
How did you react?
Was it hard or easy?

3. Evaluate the experience. Examples of questions you can ask are:

What changed as a result?
What helped?

4. Notice your bodily sensations. Examples of questions you can ask are:

What did you feel?
Were your neck muscles relaxed or tense?
How about your stomach? Other?

5. Apply the experience for future consideration. Examples of questions you can ask are:

What are the next steps?
What are helpful recommendations?
How will you use this knowledge?

It's best to do the ARENA process *in writing.*

To learn more about Jim Wales' class or to enroll, email him at jwales@sdccd.edu.

90892842R00212

Made in the USA
San Bernardino, CA
15 October 2018